THE "OSLO" MODELING LANGUAGE

DRAFT SPECIFICATION - OCTOBER 2008

David Langworthy, Brad Lovering, and Don Box

✦✦Addison-Wesley

Upper Saddle River, NJ • Boston • Indianapolis • San Francisco
New York • Toronto • Montreal • London • Munich • Paris • Madrid
Capetown • Sydney • Tokyo • Singapore • Mexico City

The publisher offers excellent discounts on this book when ordered in quantity for bulk purchases or special sales, which may include electronic versions and/or custom covers and content particular to your business, training goals, marketing focus, and branding interests. For more information, please contact:

> U.S. Corporate and Government Sales
> (800) 382-3419
> corpsales@pearsontechgroup.com

For sales outside the United States please contact:

> International Sales
> international@pearson.com

Visit us on the Web: informit.com/aw

Library of Congress Cataloging-in-Publication Data

Langworthy, David, 1964-
  The Oslo modeling language : draft specification / David Langworthy, Brad Lovering, Don Box.
    p. cm.
  Includes index.
  ISBN 0-321-60635-3 (pbk. : alk. paper) 1. Programming languages (Electronic computers) I. Lovering, Brad, 1966- II. Box, Don, 1962- III. Title.

  QA76.7.L365 2008
  005.1—dc22

                          2008039970

Microsoft is a registered trademark of Microsoft Corporation

ISBN-13: 978-0-321-60635-8
ISBN-10: 0-321-60635-3

Text printed in the United States on recycled paper at Courier in Stoughton, Massachusetts. First printing October 2008

CONTENTS AT A GLANCE

TABLE OF CONTENTS

PREFACE

Codename "Oslo" is the name of the first release of Microsoft's modeling platform. Oslo was created to simplify the process of developing, deploying, and managing software. The fundamental premise of Oslo is to reduce the gap between the intention of the developer and the artifacts that are deployed and executed. The approach used by Oslo is to allow software to be expressed as transparent and dynamic data rather than as opaque and static code. We refer to the data that defines a piece of software as a *model*. In Oslo, models are captured as structured data that is present throughout the software lifecycle. What makes Oslo unique is the fact that applications and services are actually defined *and executed* based on their models. That is, platform components read modeling information at runtime to control the behavior of an application or service. The idea is that there is no "code-spit" phase in which source code and modeling information get out of sync—rather, the model *is* the truth as far as the runtime is concerned.

The ability to define and execute programs in terms of data is one distinguishing characteristic of Oslo. Another distinguishing characteristic is the approach to making modeling information accessible to people. Oslo includes a graphical tool for creating, viewing, and updating modeling information that provides a uniform diagrammatic design surface. For many situations, diagrams are the best way for people to interact with data. However, there are also many situations (and many people) for which text is the best way to think about and work with information. That is the motivation for the "Oslo" modeling language (known as Codename "M" or just M).

M is a language for defining domain models and languages. (The latter are often referred to as *textual DSLs*.) An M domain model defines schemas and projections over structured data. An M domain language defines transformations between linear text and structured data. Both M models and languages share a common underlying data model for structured data that is compatible with relational stores such as SQL.

Part I of this book describes the domain model and language components from a pre-release version of M (specifically, the October 2008 version of the language). Part II of this document describes the textual modeling language M_g (again, the October 2008 version of the language).

For updates and errata to this specification, please refer to http://msdn.microsoft.com/oslo.

Acknowledgments

Significant contributions to this specification came from Jeffrey Schlimmer, who contributed the first draft of the simple type specification, and to Chris Sells, who applied his editorial and PM skills to turn the initial Word document into dead trees. Thanks also go to Karen Gettman at Pearson/AW for her seemingly endless patience, and to Stephan Danton for his mastery over pixels and bits.

The following individuals provided extensive comments that improved the readability (and accuracy) of this document: Michael Coulson, John Doty, John Hamby, Kris Horrocks, Leslie Lamport, Chris Sells, Don Spencer, Ralph Squillace, Janie Storkel, Clemens Szyperski, Michael Weinhardt, Bruce Williams, Scott Wiltamuth, and Matt Winkler. Thanks also go to the entire team that produces the M language framework, compiler, and runtime for backing this specification up with the always important running code.

Finally, M grew out of a community of users and developers and has been significantly influenced and improved based on their experiences and feedback. The most vocal of that community were Sonu Arora, Mohsen Agsen, Lonny Bastien, Gavin Bierman, Anthony Bloesch, Jonas Boli, Jim Carley, Yann Christensen, Steve Cook, Christopher Garg, Nikhil George, Chris Gillum, Andy Gordon, Destry Hood, Sid Jayadevan, Jim Johnson, John Justice, Geoffrey Kizer, Wojtek Kozaczynski, Kevin Lam, John Lambert, Steve Maine, Will Manis, Laurent Mollicone, Tapas Nayak, David Noble, Savas Parastatidis, Ram Raghavendra Rao, Daniel Roth, Igor Sedukhin, Joe Sharp, Prasad Sripathi Panditharadhya, Clemens Vasters, Omar Venado Estrada, Florian Voss, Tony Williams, and Eric Zinda.

About the Authors

David Langworthy, **Brad Lovering**, and **Don Box** are developers on Microsoft's "Oslo" project and were the original three members of the M language team. David, Brad, and Don have worked together on languages, protocols, and runtimes, most recently on the Windows Communication Foundation (WCF).

PART I

"OSLO" MODELING LANGUAGE SPECIFICATION

CHAPTER 1

INTRODUCTION TO "M"

The "Oslo" Modeling Language (M) is a modern, declarative language for working with data. M lets users write down how they want to structure and query their data using a convenient textual syntax that is convenient to both author and read.

M does not mandate how data is stored or accessed, nor does it mandate a specific implementation technology. Rather, M was designed to allow users to write down *what* they want from their data without having to specify *how* those desires are met against a given technology or platform. That stated, M in no way prohibits implementations from providing rich declarative or imperative support for controlling how M constructs are represented and executed in a given environment.

M builds on three basic concepts: values, types, and extents. Here's how M defines these three concepts:

1. A value is simply data that conforms to the rules of the M language.
2. A type describes a set of values.
3. An extent provides dynamic storage for values.

In general, M separates the typing of data from the storage/extent of the data. A given type can be used to describe data from multiple extents as well as to describe the results of a calculation. This allows users to start writing down types first and decide where to put or calculate the corresponding values later.

On the topic of determining where to put values, the M language does not specify how an implementation maps a declared extent to an external store such as an RDBMS. However, M was designed to make such implementations possible and is compatible with the relational model.

Another important aspect of data management that M does not address is that of update. M is a functional language that does not have constructs for changing the contents of an extent. How data changes is outside the scope of the language. That said, M anticipates that the contents of an extent can change via external (to M) stimuli. Subsequent versions of M are expected to provide declarative constructs for updating data.

This chapter provides a non-normative introduction to the fundamental concepts in M. Chapters 2-6 provide the normative definition of the language.

1.1 Values

The easiest way to get started with M is to look at some values. M has intrinsic support for constructing values. The following is a legal value in M:

```
"Hello, world"
```

The quotation marks tell M that this is the text value `Hello, world`. M literals can also be numbers. The following literal:

```
1
```

is the numeric value one. Finally, there are two literals that represent logical values:

```
true
false
```

We've just seen examples of using literals to write down textual, numeric, and logical values. We can also use expressions to write down values that are computed.

An M expression applies an *operator* to zero or more *operands* to produce a *result*. An operator is either a built-in operator (e.g., +) or a user-defined function (which we look at in Section 1.2.5). An *operand* is a value that is used by the operator to calculate the *result* of the expression, which is itself a value. Expressions nest, so the operands themselves can be expressions.

M defines two equality operators: equals, ==, and not equals, !=, both of which result in either `true` or `false` based on the equivalence/nonequivalence of the two operands. Here are some expressions that use the equality operators:

```
1 == 1
"Hello" != "hELLO"
true != false
```

All of these expressions will yield the value `true` when evaluated.

M defines the standard four relational operators, less-than <, greater-than >, less-than-or-equal <=, and greater-than-or-equal >=, which work over numeric and textual values. M also defines the standard three logical operators: and `&&`, or `||`, and not `!` that combine logical values.

The following expressions show these operators in action:

```
1 < 4
1 == 1
1 < 4 != 1 > 4
!(1 + 1 == 3)
(1 + 1 == 3) || (2 + 2 < 10)
(1 + 1 == 2) && (2 + 2 < 10)
```

Again, all of these expressions yield the value `true` when evaluated.

1.1.1 Collections

All of the values we saw in the previous section were *simple* values. In M, a simple value is a value that has no uniform way to be decomposed into constituent parts. While there are textual operators that allow you to extract substrings from a text value, those operators are specific to textual data and don't work on numeric data. Similarly, any "bit-level" operations on binary values don't apply to text or numeric data.

An M *collection* is a value that groups together zero or more *elements* that themselves are values. We can write down collections in expressions using an *initializer,* `{ }`.

The following expressions each use an initializer to yield a collection value:

```
{ 1, 2 }
{ 1 }
{ }
```

As with simple values, the equivalence operators `==` and `!=` are defined over collections. In M, two collections are considered equivalent if and only if each element has a distinct equivalent element in the other collection. That allows us to write the following equivalence expressions:

```
{ 1, 2 } == { 1, 2 }
{ 1, 2 } != { 1 }
```

both of which are true.

The elements of a collection can consist of different kinds of values:

```
{ true, "Hello" }
```

and these values can be the result of arbitrary calculation:

```
{ 1 + 2, 99 - 3, 4 < 9 }
```

which is equivalent to the collection:

```
{ 3, 96, true }.
```

The order of elements in a collection is not significant. That means that the following expression is also true:

```
{ 1, 2 } == { 2, 1 }
```

Finally, collections can contain duplicate elements, which are significant. That makes the following expression:

```
{ 1, 2, 2 } != { 1, 2 }
```

also true.

M defines a set of built-in operators that are specific to collections. The most important is the in operator, which tests whether a given value is an element of the collection. The result of the in operator is a logical value that indicates whether the value is or is not an element of the collection. For example, these expressions:

```
1 in { 1, 2, 3 }
!(1 in { "Hello", 9 })
```

both result in true.

M defines a Count member on collections that calculates the number of elements in a collection. This use of that operator:

```
{ 1, 2, 2, 3 }.Count
```

results in the value 4. The postfix # operator returns the count of a collection, so

```
{ 1, 2, 2, 3 }# == { 1, 2, 2, 3 }.Count
```

returns `true`.

As noted earlier, M collections may contain duplicates. You can apply the `Distinct` member to get a version of the collection with any duplicates removed:

```
{ 1, 2, 3, 1 }.Distinct == { 1, 2, 3 }
```

The result of `Distinct` is not just a collection but is also a set, that is, a collection of distinct elements.

M also defines set union `"|"` and set intersection `"&"` operators, which also yield sets:

```
({ 1, 2, 3, 1 } | { 1, 2, 4 }) == { 1, 2, 3, 4 }
({ 1, 2, 3, 1 } & { 1, 2, 4 }) == { 1, 2 }
```

Note that union and intersection always return collections that are sets, even when applied to collections that contain duplicates.

M defines the subset and superset using `<=` and `>=`. Again these operations convert collections to sets. The following expressions evaluate to `true`.

```
{ 1, 2 } <= { 1, 2, 3 }
{ "Hello", "World" } >= { "World" }
{ 1, 2, 1 } <= { 1, 2, 3 }
```

Arguably the most commonly used collection operator is the `where` operator. The `where` operator applies a logical expression (called the *predicate*) to each element in a collection (called the *domain*) and results in a new collection that consists of only the elements for which the predicate holds true. To allow the element to be used in the predicate, the `where` operator introduces the symbol `value` to stand in for the specific element being tested.

For example, consider this expression that uses a `where` operator:

```
{ 1, 2, 3, 4, 5, 6 } where value > 3
```

In this example, the domain is the collection `{ 1, 2, 3, 4, 5, 6 }` and the predicate is the expression `value > 3`. Note that the identifier `value` is available only within the scope of the predicate expression. The result of this expression is the collection `{ 4, 5, 6 }`.

M supports a richer set of query comprehensions using a syntax similar to that of Language Integrated Query (LINQ). For example, the `where` example just shown can be written in long form as follows:

```
from value in { 1, 2, 3, 4, 5, 6 }
where value > 3
select value
```

In general, M supports the LINQ operators with these significant exceptions:

1. ElementAt/First/Last/Range/Skip are not supported—M collections are unordered and do not support positional access to elements.
2. Reverse is not supported—Again, position is not significant on M collections.
3. Take/TakeWhile/Single—These operators do not exist in M.
4. Choose—This selects an arbitrary element.
5. ToArray/ToDictionary/ToList—There are no corresponding CLR types in M.
6. Cast-typing works differently in M—You can achieve the same effect using a where operator.

While the `where` operator allows elements to be accessed based on a calculation over the values of each element, there are situations where it would be much more convenient to simply assign names to each element and then access the element values by its assigned name. M defines a distinct kind of value called an *entity* for just this purpose.

1.1.2 Entities

An *entity* consists of zero or more name-value pairs called *fields*. Entities can be constructed in M using an initializer. Here's a simple entity value:

```
{ X = 100, Y = 200 }
```

This entity has two fields: one named x with the value of 100, the other named y with the value of 200.
Entity initializers can use arbitrary expressions as field values:

```
{ X = 50 + 50, Y = 300 - 100 }
```

And the names of members can be arbitrary Unicode text:

```
{
  [Horizontal Coordinate] = 100,
  [Vertical Coordinate] = 200
}
```

If the member name matches the Identifier pattern, it can be written without the surrounding [ ]. An identifier must begin with an upper or lowercase letter or "_" and be followed by a sequence of letters, digits, "_", and "$".

Here are a few examples:

```
HelloWorld = 1       // matches the Identifier pattern
[Hello World] = 1    // doesn't match identifier pattern
_HelloWorld = 1      // matches the Identifier pattern
A = 1                // matches the Identifier pattern
[1] = 1              // doesn't match identifier pattern
```

It is always legal to use [ ] to escape symbolic names; however, most of the examples in this document use names that don't require escaping and, therefore, do not use escaping syntax for readability.

M imposes no limitations on the values of entity members. It is legal for the value of an entity member to refer to another entity:

```
{
  TopLeft = { X = 100, Y = 200 },
  BottomRight = { X = 400, Y = 100 }
}
```

or a collection:

```
{
  LotteryPicks = { 1, 18, 25, 32, 55, 61 },
  Odds = 0.00000001
}
```

or a collection of entities:

```
{
  Color = "Red",
  Path = {
    { X = 100, Y = 100 },
```

```
    { X = 200, Y = 200 },
    { X = 300, Y = 100 },
    { X = 300, Y = 100 },
  }
}
```

This last example illustrates that entity values are legal for use as elements in collections.

Entity initializers are useful for constructing new entity values. M defines the dot, ".", operator over entities for accessing the value of a given member. For example, this expression:

```
{ X = 100, Y = 200 }.X
```

yields the value of the x member, which in this case is 100. The result of the dot operator is just a value that is subject to subsequent operations. For example, this expression:

```
{ Center = { X = 100, Y = 200 }, Radius = 3 }.Center.Y
```

yields the value 200.

1.2 Types

Expressions give us a great way to write down how to *calculate* values based on other values. Often, we want to write down how to *categorize* values for the purposes of validation or allocation. In M, we categorize values using types.

An M type describes a collection of acceptable or *conformant* values. We use types to constrain which values may appear in a particular context (for example, an operand, a storage location).

With a few notable exceptions, M allows types to be used as collections. For example, we can use the in operator to test whether a value conforms to a given type. The following expressions are true:

```
1 in Number
"Hello, world" in Text
```

Note that the names of the built-in types are available directly in the M language. We can introduce new names for types using type declarations. For example, this type declaration introduces the type name My Text as a synonym for the Text simple type:

```
type [My Text] : Text;
```

With this type name now available, we can write the following:

```
"Hello, world" in [My Text]
```

Note that the name of the type [My Text] contains spaces and is subject to the same escaping rules as the member names in entities.

While it is moderately useful to introduce your own names for an existing type, it's far more useful to apply a predicate to the underlying type:

```
type SmallText : Text where value.Count < 7;
```

In this example, we've constrained the universe of possible Text values to those in which the value contains less than seven characters. That means that the following holds true:

```
"Terse" in SmallText
!("Verbose" in SmallText)
```

Type declarations compose:

```
type TinyText : SmallText where value.Count < 6;
```

The preceding is equivalent to the following:

```
type TinyText : Text where value.Count < 6;
```

It's important to note that the name of the type exists so an M declaration or expression can refer to it. We can assign any number of names to the same type (for example, Text where value.Count < 7) and a given value either conforms to all of them or to none of them. For example, consider this example:

```
type A : Number where value < 100;
type B : Number where value < 100;
```

Given these two type definitions, both of the following expressions will evaluate to true:

```
1 in A
1 in B
```

If we introduce the following third type:

```
type C : Number where value > 0;
```

we can also state this:

```
1 in C
```

In M, types are sets of values, and it is possible to define a new type by explicitly enumerating those values:

```
type PrimaryColors { "Red", "Blue", "Yellow" }
```

This is how an enumeration is defined in M. Any type in M is a collection of values. For example, the types `Logical` and `Integer8` defined next could be defined as the collections:

```
{ true, false }
{-128, -127, ..., -1, 0, 1, ..., 127}
```

A general principle of M is that a given value may conform to any number of types. This is a departure from the way many object-based systems work, in which a value is bound to a specific type at initialization-time and is a member of the finite set of subtypes that were specified when the type was defined.

One last type-related operation bears discussion—the type ascription operator ":". The type ascription operator asserts that a given value conforms to a specific type.

In general, when we see values in expressions, M has some notion of the expected type of that value based on the declared result type for the operator or function being applied. For example, the result of the logical and operator "`&&`" is declared to be conformant with type `Logical`.

It is occasionally useful (or even required) to apply additional constraints to a given value—typically to use that value in another context that has differing requirements.

For example, consider the following simple type definition:

```
type SuperPositive : Number where value > 5;
```

And let's now assume that there's a function named `CalcIt` that is declared to accept a value of type `SuperPositive` as an operand. We'd like M to allow expressions like this:

```
CalcIt(20)
CalcIt(42 + 99)
```

and prohibit expressions like this:

```
CalcIt(-1)
CalcIt(4)
```

In fact, M does exactly what we want for these four examples. This is because these expressions express their operands in terms of simple built-in operators over constants. All of the information needed to determine the validity of the expressions is readily and cheaply available the moment the M source text for the expression is encountered.

However, if the expression draws upon dynamic sources of data or user-defined functions, we must use the type ascription operator to assert that a value will conform to a given type.

To understand how the type ascription operator works with values, let's assume that there is a second function, GetVowelCount, that is declared to accept an operand of type Text and return a value of type Number that indicates the number of vowels in the operand.

Since we can't know based on the declaration of GetVowelCount whether its results will be greater than five or not, the following expression is not a legal M expression:

```
CalcIt( GetVowelCount(someTextVariable) )
```

Because GetVowelCount's declared result type Number includes values that do not conform to the declared operand type of CalcIt, which is SuperPositive, M assumes that this expression was written in error and will refuse to even attempt to evaluate the expression.

When we rewrite this expression to the following legal expression using the type ascription operator:

```
CalcIt( GetVowelCount(someTextVariable) : SuperPositive )
```

we are telling M that we have enough understanding of the GetVowelCount function to know that we'll always get a value that conforms to the type SuperPositive. In short, we're telling M we know what we're doing.

But what if we don't? What if we misjudged how the GetVowelCount function works and a particular evaluation results in a negative number? Because the CalcIt function was declared to accept only values that conform to `SuperPositive`, the system will ensure that all values passed to it are greater than five. To ensure this constraint is never violated, the system may need to inject a dynamic constraint test that has a potential to fail when evaluated. This failure will not occur when the M source text is first processed (as was the case with `CalcIt(-1)`)—rather it will occur when the expression is actually evaluated.

Here's the general principle at play.

M implementations will typically attempt to report any constraint violations before the first expression is evaluated. This is called *static* enforcement, and implementations will manifest this much like a syntax error. However, as we've seen, some constraints can only be enforced against live data and, therefore, require *dynamic* enforcement.

In general, the M philosophy is to make it easy for users to write down their intention and put the burden on the M implementation to "make it work." However, to allow a particular M program to be used in diverse environments, a fully featured M implementation should be configurable to reject M program that rely on dynamic enforcement for correctness to reduce the performance and operational costs of dynamic constraint violations.

1.2.1 Collection Types

M defines a *type constructor* for specifying collection types. The collection type constructor restricts the *type* and *count* of elements a collection may contain. All collection types are restrictions over the intrinsic type `Collection`, which all collection values conform to:

```
{ } in Collection
{ 1, false } in Collection
! ("Hello" in Collection)
```

The last example is interesting, in that it illustrates that the collection types do not overlap with the simple types. There is no value that conforms to both a collection type and a simple type.

A collection type constructor specifies both the type of element and the acceptable element count. The element count is typically specified using one of the three operators:

```
T* - zero or more Ts
T+ - one or more Ts
T#m..n - between m and n Ts
```

The collection type constructors can either use operators or be written longhand as a constraint over the intrinsic type `Collection`:

```
type SomeNumbers : Number+;
type TwoToFourNumbers : Number#2..4;
type ThreeNumbers : Number#3;
type FourOrMoreNumbers : Number#4..;
```

These types describe the same sets of values as these longhand definitions:

```
type SomeNumbers : Collection where value.Count >= 1
                                  && item in Number;
type TwoToFourNumbers : Collection where value.Count >= 2
                                  && value.Count <= 4
                                  && item in Number;
type ThreeNumbers : Collection where value.Count == 3
                                  && item in Number;
type FourOrMoreNumbers : Collection where value.Count >= 4
                                  && item in Number;
```

In the case that `value` itself is a collection, an additional variable `item` is introduced into scope. The `item` variable ranges over the elements of `value` (which must be a collection). Clauses that use `item` must hold for every element of `value`.

Independent of which form is used to declare the types, we can now assert the following hold:

```
!({ } in TwoToFourNumbers)
!({ "One", "Two", "Three" } in TwoToFourNumbers)
{ 1, 2, 3 } in TwoToFourNumbers
{ 1, 2, 3 } in ThreeNumbers
{ 1, 2, 3, 4, 5 } in FourOrMoreNumbers
```

The collection type constructors compose with the `where` operator, allowing the following type check to succeed:

```
{ 1, 2 } in (Number where value < 3)*
  where value.Count % 2 == 0
```

Note that the `where` inside the parentheses applies to elements of the collection, and the `where` outside the parentheses operator applies to the collection itself.

1.2.2 Nullable Types

We have seen many useful values: `42`, `"Hello"`, `{1,2,3}`. The distinguished value `null` serves as a placeholder for some other value that is not known. A type with `null` in the value space is called a nullable type. The value `null` can be added to the value space of a type with an explicit union of the type and a collection containing null or using the postfix operator `?`. The following expressions are true:

```
! (null in Integer)
null in Integer?
null in (Integer | { null } )
```

The `??` operator converts between a null value and known value:

```
null ?? 1 == 1
3 ?? 1 == 3
```

Arithmetic operations on a null operand return null:

```
1 + null == null
null * 3 == null
```

Logical operators, conditional, and constraints require non-nullable operands.

1.2.3 Entity Types

Just as we can use the collection type constructors to specify what kinds of collections are valid in a given context, we can do the same for entities using entity types.

An entity type declares the expected members for a set of entity values. The members of an entity type can be declared either as *fields* or as *computed values*. The value of a field is stored; a computed value is evaluated. All entity types are restrictions over the `Entity` type.

Here is the simplest entity type:

```
type MyEntity : Language.Entity;
```

The type `MyEntity` does not declare any fields. In M, entity types are *open* in that entity values that conform to the type may contain fields whose names are not declared in the type. That means that the following type test:

```
{ X = 100, Y = 200 } in MyEntity
```

will evaluate to true, as the MyEntity type says nothing about fields named x and y.

Most entity types contain one or more field declarations. At a minimum, a field declaration states the name of the expected field:

```
type Point { X; Y; }
```

This type definition describes the set of entities that contain *at least* fields named x and y irrespective of the values of those fields. That means that the following type tests will all evaluate to true:

```
{ X = 100, Y = 200 } in Point

// more fields than expected OK
{ X = 100, Y = 200, Z = 300 } in Point

// not enough fields - not OK
! ({ X = 100 } in Point)

{ X = true, Y = "Hello, world" } in Point
```

The last example demonstrates that the Point type does not constrain the values of the x and y fields—any value is allowed. We can write a new type that constrains the values of x and y to numeric values:

```
type NumericPoint {
   X : Number;
   Y : Number where value > 0;
}
```

Note that we're using type ascription syntax to assert that the value of the x and y fields must conform to the type Number. With this in place, the following expressions all evaluate to true:

```
{ X = 100, Y = 200 } in NumericPoint
{ X = 100, Y = 200, Z = 300 } in NumericPoint
! ({ X = true, Y = "Hello, world" } in NumericPoint)
! ({ X = 0, Y = 0 } in NumericPoint)
```

As we saw in the discussion of simple types, the name of the type exists only so that M declarations and expressions can refer to it. That is why both of the following type tests succeed:

```
{ X = 100, Y = 200 } in NumericPoint
{ X = 100, Y = 200 } in Point
```

even though the definitions of NumericPoint and Point are independent.

1.2.4 Declaring Fields

Fields are named units of storage that hold values. M allows you to initialize the value of a field as part of an entity initializer. However, M does not specify any mechanism for changing the value of a field once it is initialized. In M, we assume that any changes to field values happen outside the scope of M.

A field declaration can indicate that there is a default value for the field. Field declarations that have a default value do not require conformant entities to have a corresponding field specified. (We sometimes call such field declarations *optional fields*.) For example, consider this type definition:

```
type Point3d {
   X : Number;
   Y : Number;
   Z = -1 : Number; // default value of negative one
}
```

Because the z field has a default value, the following type test will succeed:

```
{ X = 100, Y = 200 } in Point3d
```

Moreover, if we apply a type ascription operator to the value:

```
({ X = 100, Y = 200 } : Point3d)
```

we can now access the Z field like this:

```
({ X = 100, Y = 200 } : Point3d).Z
```

This expression will yield the value -1.

If a field declaration does not have a corresponding default value, conformant entities must specify a value for that field. Default values are typically written down using the explicit syntax shown for the z field of Point3d. If the type of a field is either nullable or a zero-to-many collection, then there is an implicit default value for the declaring field of `null` for optional and `{}` for the collection.

For example, consider this type:

```
type PointND {
   X : Number;
   Y : Number;
   Z : Number?;          // Z is optional
   BeyondZ : Number*;    // BeyondZ is optional too
}
```

Again, the following type test will succeed:

```
{ X = 100, Y = 200 } in PointND
```

and ascribing the `PointND` to the value will allow us to get these defaults:

```
({ X = 100, Y = 200 } : PointND).Z == null
({ X = 100, Y = 200 } : PointND).BeyondZ == { }
```

The choice of using a nullable type versus an explicit default value to model optional fields typically comes down to style.

1.2.5 Declaring Computed Values

Calculated values are named expressions whose values are computed rather than stored. Here's an example of a type that declares a computed value, `IsHigh`:

```
type PointPlus {
   X : Number;

   Y : Number;

// a computed value

   IsHigh() : Logical { Y > 0 }

}
```

Note that unlike field declarations which end in a semicolon, computed value declarations end with the expression surrounded by braces.

Like field declarations, a computed value declaration may omit the type ascription, as this example does:

```
type PointPlus {
  X : Number;
  Y : Number;
// a computed value with no type ascription
  InMagicQuadrant() { IsHigh && X > 0 }
  IsHigh() : Logical { Y > 0 }
}
```

When no type is explicitly ascribed to a computed value, M will infer the type automatically based on the declared result type of the underlying expression. In this example, because the logical-and operator used in the expression was declared as returning a `Logical`, the `InMagicQuadrant` computed value also is ascribed to yield a `Logical` value.

The two computed values we just defined and used didn't require any additional information to calculate their results other than the entity value itself. A computed value may optionally declare a list of named parameters whose actual values must be specified when using the computed value in an expression. Here's an example of a computed value that requires parameters:

```
type PointPlus {
  X : Number;
  Y : Number;
  // a computed value that requires a parameter
  WithinBounds(radius : Number) : Logical {
    X * X + Y * Y <= radius * radius
  }
  InMagicQuadrant() { IsHigh && X > 0 }
  IsHigh() : Logical { Y > 0 }
}
```

To use this computed value in an expression, you must provide values for the parameters:

```
({ X = 100, Y = 200 } : PointPlus).WithinBounds(50)
```

When calculating the value of WithinBounds, M will bind the value 50 to the symbol radius—this will cause the WithinBounds computed value to evaluate to false.

It is useful to note that both computed values and default values for fields are part of the type definition, not part of the values that conform to the type. For example, consider these three type definitions:

```
type Point {
  X : Number;
  Y : Number;
}
type RichPoint {
  X : Number;
  Y : Number;
  Z = -1 : Number;
  IsHigh() : Logical { X < Y }
}
type WeirdPoint {
  X : Number;
  Y : Number;
  Z = 42 : Number;
  IsHigh() : Logical { false }
}
```

Because RichPoint and WeirdPoint have only two required fields (x and y), we can state the following:

```
{ X=1, Y=2 } in RichPoint
{ X=1, Y=2 } in WeirdPoint
```

However, the IsHigh computed value is only available when we ascribe one of these two types to the entity value:

```
({ X=1, Y=2 } : RichPoint).IsHigh == true
({ X=1, Y=2 } : WeirdPoint).IsHigh == false
```

Because IsHigh is purely part of the type and not the value, when we chain the ascription like this:

```
(({ X=1, Y=2 } : RichPoint) : WeirdPoint).IsHigh == false
```

the outer-most ascription that determines which function is called.

A similar principle is at play with respect to how default values work. Again, the default value is part of the type, not the entity value. When we write the following expression:

```
({ X=1, Y=2 } : RichPoint).Z == -1
```

the underlying entity value still only contains two field values (1 and 2 for x and y respectively). Where default values differ from computed values is when we chain ascriptions. Consider this expression:

```
(({ X=1, Y=2 } : RichPoint) : WeirdPoint).Z == -1
```

Because the RichPoint ascription is applied first, the resultant entity has a field named z whose value is -1; however, there is no storage allocated for the value. (It's part of the type's interpretation of the value.) When we apply the WeirdPoint ascription, we're applying it to the result of the first ascription, which does have a field named z, so that value is used to specify the value for z—the default value specified by WeirdPoint is not needed.

1.2.6 Constraints on Entity Types

Like all types, a constraint may be applied to an entity type using the where operator. Consider the following type definition:

```
type HighPoint {
   X : Number;
   Y : Number;
} where X < Y;
```

In this example, all values that conform to the type HighPoint are guaranteed to have an x value that is less than the y value. That means that the following expressions:

```
{ X = 100, Y = 200 } in HighPoint
! ({ X = 300, Y = 200 } in HighPoint)
```

both evaluate to true.

Now consider the following type definitions:

```
type Point {
   X : Number;
   Y : Number;
```

```
}
type Visual {
   Opacity : Number;
}
type VisualPoint {
   DotSize : Number;
} where value in Point && value in Visual;
```

The third type, `VisualPoint`, names the set of entity values that have at least the numeric fields `X`, `Y`, `Opacity`, and `DotSize`.

Because it is a common desire to factor member declarations into smaller pieces that can be easily composed, M provides explicit syntax support for this. We can rewrite the `VisualPoint` type definition using that syntax:

```
type VisualPoint : Point, Visual {
   DotSize : Number;
}
```

To be clear, this is just shorthand for the preceding long-hand definition that used a constraint expression. Both of these definitions are equivalent to this even longer-hand definition:

```
type VisualPoint {
   X : Number;
   Y : Number;
   Opacity : Number;
   DotSize : Number;
}
```

Again, the names of the types are just ways to refer to types—the values themselves have no record of the type names used to describe them.

1.3 Queries

M extends LINQ query comprehensions with several features to make authoring simple queries more concise. The keywords, `where` and `select` are available as binary infix operators. Also, indexers are automatically added to strongly typed collections. These features allow common queries to be authored more compactly as illustrated next.

1.3.1 Filtering

Filtering extracts elements from an existing collection. Consider the following collection:

```
People {
   { First = "Mary", Last = "Smith", Age = 24 },
   { First = "John", Last = "Doe", Age = 32 },
   { First = "Dave", Last = "Smith", Age = 32 },
}
```

This query extracts people with `Age == 32` from the `People` collection:

```
from p in People
where p.Age == 32
select p
```

An equivalent query can be written with either of the following expressions:

```
People where value.Age == 32
People.Age(32)
```

The `where` operator takes a collection on the left and a Logical expression on the right. The `where` operator introduces a keyword identifier `value` into the scope of the Logical expression that is bound to each member of the collection. The resulting collection contains the members for which the expression is true. The expression:

```
Collection where Expression
```

is exactly equivalent to:

```
from value in Collection
where Expression
select value
```

Collection types gain *indexer* members that correspond to the fields of their corresponding element type. That is, this:

```
Collection . Field ( Expression )
```

is equivalent to:

```
from value in Collection
where Field == Expression
select value
```

1.3.2 Selection

Select is also available as an infix operator. Consider the following simple query:

```
from p in People
select p.First + p.Last
```

This computes the select expression over each member of the collection and returns the result. Using the infix `select` it can be written equivalently as:

```
People select value.First + value.Last
```

The `select` operator takes a collection on the left and an arbitrary expression on the right. As with `where`, `select` introduces the keyword identifier `value` that ranges over each element in the collection. The `select` operator maps the expression over each element in the collection and returns the result. The expression:

```
Collection select Expression
```

Is exactly equivalent to:

```
from value in Collection
select Expression
```

A trivial use of the select operator is to extract a single field:

```
People select value.First
```

Collections are augmented with accessors to fields that can be extracted directly. For example `People.First` yields a new collection containing all the first names, and `People.Last` yields a collection with all the last names.

1.4 Modules

All of the examples shown so far have been "loose M" that is taken out of context. To write a legal M program, all source text must appear in the context of a *module definition*. A module defines a top-level namespace for any type names that are defined. A module also defines a scope for defining extents that will store actual values, as well as computed values.

Here is a simple module definition:

```
module Geometry {
  // declare a type
  type Point {
    X : Integer; Y : Integer;
  }
  // declare some extents
  Points : Point*;
  Origin : Point;

  // declare a computed value
  TotalPointCount { Points.Count + 1; }
}
```

In this example, the module defines one type named `Geometry.Point`. This type describes what point values will look like, but doesn't mention any locations where those values can be stored.

This example also includes two module-scoped extents (Points and Origin). Module-scoped field declarations are identical in syntax to those used in entity types. However, fields declared in an entity type simply name the *potential* for storage once an extent has been determined; in contrast, fields declared at module-scope name *actual* storage that must be mapped by an implementation to load and interpret the module.

Modules may refer to declarations in other modules by using an *import directive* to name the module containing the referenced declarations. For a declaration to be referenced by other modules, the declaration must be explicitly exported using an *export directive.*

Consider this module:

```
module MyModule {
  import HerModule; // declares HerType

  export MyType1;
  export MyExtent1;

  type MyType1 : Logical*;
  type MyType2 : HerType;
  MyExtent1 : Number*;
  MyExtent2 : HerType;
}
```

Note that only `MyType1` and `MyExtent1` are visible to other modules. This makes the following definition of `HerModule` legal:

```
module HerModule {
  import MyModule; // declares MyType1 and MyExtent1
  export HerType;

  type HerType : Text where value.Count < 100;
  type Private : Number where !(value in MyExtent1);
  SomeStorage : MyType1;
}
```

As this example shows, modules may have circular dependencies.

CHAPTER 2

LEXICAL STRUCTURE

2.1 Programs

An M program consists of one or more source files, known formally as compilation units. A compilation unit file is an ordered sequence of Unicode characters. Compilation units typically have a one-to-one correspondence with files in a file system, but this correspondence is not required. For maximal portability, it is recommended that files in a file system be encoded with the UTF-8 encoding.

Conceptually speaking, a program is compiled using four steps:

1. Lexical analysis, which translates a stream of Unicode input characters into a stream of tokens. Lexical analysis evaluates and executes pre-processing directives.
2. Syntactic analysis, which translates the stream of tokens into an abstract syntax tree.
3. Semantic analysis, which resolves all symbols in the abstract syntax tree, type checks the structure, and generates a semantic graph.
4. Code generation, which generates an image from the semantic graph. An image is a list of executable instructions for some target runtime, for example, SQL Server.

Further tools may link images and load them into a runtime.

2.2 Grammars

This specification presents the syntax of the M programming language using two grammars. The lexical grammar defines how Unicode characters are combined to form line terminators, white space, comments, tokens, and pre-processing directives. The syntactic grammar defines how the tokens resulting from the lexical grammar are combined to form M programs.

2.2.1 Grammar Notation

The lexical and syntactic grammars are presented using grammar productions. Each grammar production defines a non-terminal symbol and the possible expansions of that non-terminal symbol into sequences of non-terminal or terminal symbols. In grammar productions, *non-terminal* symbols are shown in italic type, and `terminal` symbols are shown in a fixed-width font.

The first line of a grammar production is the name of the non-terminal symbol being defined, followed by a colon. Each successive indented line contains a possible expansion of the non-terminal given as a sequence of non-terminal or terminal symbols. For example, the production:

IdentifierVerbatim:

   [*IdentifierVerbatimCharacters*]

defines an *IdentifierVerbatim* to consist of the token "[", followed by *IdentifierVerbatimCharacters*, followed by the token "]".

When there is more than one possible expansion of a non-terminal symbol, the alternatives are listed on separate lines. For example, the production:

DecimalDigits:

   DecimalDigit

   DecimalDigits DecimalDigit

defines *DecimalDigits* to either consist of a *DecimalDigit* or consist of *DecimalDigits* followed by a *DecimalDigit*. In other words, the definition is recursive and specifies that decimal digits list consists of one or more decimal digits.

A subscripted suffix *"opt"* is used to indicate an optional symbol. The production:

DecimalLiteral:

   IntegerLiteral . DecimalDigit DecimalDigits$_{opt}$

is shorthand for:

DecimalLiteral:

   IntegerLiteral . DecimalDigit

   IntegerLiteral . DecimalDigit DecimalDigits

and defines an *DecimalLiteral* to consist of an *IntegerLiteral* followed by a "." a *DecimalDigit* and by optional *DecimalDigits*.

Alternatives are normally listed on separate lines, though in cases where there are many alternatives, the phrase "one of" may precede a list of expansions given on a single line. This is simply shorthand for listing each of the alternatives on a separate line. For example, the production:

Sign: one of

   +   −

is shorthand for:

Sign:

   +

   −

Conversely, exclusions are designated with the phrase "none of." For example, the production

TextSimple: none of

   "

   \

NewLineCharacter

permits all characters except '"', '\', and new line characters.

2.2.2 Lexical Grammar

The lexical grammar of M is presented in 2.3. The terminal symbols of the lexical grammar are the characters of the Unicode character set, and the lexical grammar specifies how characters are combined to form tokens, white space, and comments (Section 2.3.2).

Every source file in an M program must conform to the *Input* production of the lexical grammar.

2.2.3 Syntactic Grammar

The syntactic grammar of M is presented in the chapters that follow this chapter. The terminal symbols of the syntactic grammar are the tokens defined by the lexical grammar, and the syntactic grammar specifies how tokens are combined to form M programs.

Every source file in an M program must conform to the *CompilationUnit* production of the syntactic grammar.

2.3 Lexical Analysis

The *Input* production defines the lexical structure of an M source file. Each source file in an M program must conform to this lexical grammar production.

Input:

   InputSection$_{opt}$

InputSection:

   InputSectionPart

   InputSection InputSectionPart

InputSectionPart:

   InputElements$_{opt}$ *NewLine*

InputElements:

   InputElement

   InputElements InputElement

InputElement:

   Whitespace

   Comment

   Token

Four basic elements make up the lexical structure of an M source file: line terminators, white space, comments, and tokens. Of these basic elements, only tokens are significant in the syntactic grammar of an M program.

The lexical processing of an M source file consists of reducing the file into a sequence of tokens that becomes the input to the syntactic analysis. Line terminators, white space, and comments can serve to separate tokens, but otherwise these lexical elements have no impact on the syntactic structure of an M program.

When several lexical grammar productions match a sequence of characters in a source file, the lexical processing always forms the longest possible lexical element. For example, the character sequence // is processed as the beginning of a single-line comment because that lexical element is longer than a single / token.

2.3.1 Line Terminators

Line terminators divide the characters of an M source file into lines.

NewLine:

  NewLineCharacter

  U+000D   U+000A

NewLineCharacter:

  U+000A   *// Line Feed*

  U+000D   *// Carriage Return*

  U+0085 *// Next Line*

  U+2028 *// Line Separator*

  U+2029 *// Paragraph Separator*

For compatibility with source code editing tools that add end-of-file markers, and to enable a source file to be viewed as a sequence of properly terminated lines, the following transformations are applied, in order, to every compilation unit:

- If the last character of the source file is a Control-Z character (U+001A), this character is deleted.
- A carriage-return character (U+000D) is added to the end of the source file if that source file is nonempty and if the last character of the source file is not a carriage return (U+000D), a line feed (U+000A), a line separator (U+2028), or a paragraph separator (U+2029).

2.3.2 Comments

Two forms of comments are supported: single-line comments and delimited comments. Single-line comments start with the characters `//` and extend to the end of the source line. Delimited comments start with the characters `/*` and end with the characters `*/`. Delimited comments may span multiple lines.

Comment:

   CommentDelimited

   CommentLine

CommentDelimited:

   `/*` *CommentDelimitedContents*$_{opt}$ `*/`

CommentDelimitedContent:

   `*` none of `/`

CommentDelimitedContents:

   CommentDelimitedContent

   CommentDelimitedContents *CommentDelimitedContent*

CommentLine:

   `//` *CommentLineContents*$_{opt}$

CommentLineContent: none of

   NewLineCharacter

CommentLineContents:

   CommentLineContent

   CommentLineContents *CommentLineContent*

Comments do not nest. The character sequences `/*` and `*/` have no special meaning within a `//` comment, and the character sequences `//` and `/*` have no special meaning within a delimited comment.

    Comments are not processed within `Text` literals.

    The example

```
// This defines a
// Person entity
//
```

```
type Person = {
    Name : Text;
    Age : Number;
}
```

shows three single-line comments.
The example

```
/* This defines a
   Person entity
*/
type Person = {
    Name : Text;
    Age : Number;
}
```

includes one delimited comment.

2.3.3 Whitespace

Whitespace is defined as any character with Unicode class Zs (which includes the space character) as well as the horizontal tab character, the vertical tab character, and the form feed character.

Whitespace:

   WhitespaceCharacters

WhitespaceCharacter:

   U+0009   *// Horizontal Tab*

   U+000B   *// Vertical Tab*

   U+000C   *// Form Feed*

   U+0020   *// Space*

   NewLineCharacter

WhitespaceCharacters:

   WhitespaceCharacter

   WhitespaceCharacters WhitespaceCharacter

2.4 Tokens

There are several kinds of tokens: identifiers, keywords, literals, operators, and punctuators. White space and comments are not tokens, though they act as separators for tokens.

Token:

   Identifier

   Keyword

   Literal

   OperatorOrPunctuator

2.4.1 Identifiers

A regular identifier begins with a letter or underscore and then any sequence of letter, underscore, dollar sign, or digit. An escaped identifier is enclosed in square brackets. It contains any sequence of Text literal characters.

Identifier:

   IdentifierBegin IdentifierCharacters$_{opt}$

   IdentifierVerbatim

IdentifierBegin:

   —

   Letter

IdentifierCharacter:

   IdentifierBegin

   $

   DecimalDigit

IdentifierCharacters:

   IdentifierCharacter

   IdentifierCharacters IdentifierCharacter

IdentifierVerbatim:

   [*IdentifierVerbatimCharacters*]

IdentifierVerbatimCharacter:

   none of]

   IdentifierVerbatimEscape

IdentifierVerbatimCharacters:

   IdentifierVerbatimCharacter

   IdentifierVerbatimCharacters IdentifierVerbatimCharacter

IdentifierVerbatimEscape:

   `\ \`

   `\ ]`

Letter:

   `a..z`

   `A..Z`

DecimalDigit:

   `0..9`

DecimalDigits:

   DecimalDigit

   DecimalDigits DecimalDigit

2.4.2 Keywords

A keyword is an identifier-like sequence of characters that is reserved and cannot be used as an identifier except when escaped with square brackets [].

Keyword:

```
accumulate

by

equals

export

from

group

identity

import
```

```
in

into

item

join

let

module

null

select

this

type

unique

value

where
```

2.4.3 Literals

A literal is a source code representation of a value.

Literal:

    DecimalLiteral

    IntegerLiteral

    ScientificLiteral

    DateTimeLiteral

    TimeLiteral

    CharacterLiteral

    TextLiteral

    BinaryLiteral

    GuidLiteral

    LogicalLiteral

    NullLiteral

Literals may be ascribed with a type to override the default type ascription.

2.4.3.1 Decimal Literals

Decimal literals are used to write fixed-point or exact number values.

DecimalLiteral:

   IntegerLiteral **.** *DecimalDigit DecimalDigits$_{opt}$*

Decimal literals default to the smallest standard library type that can contain the value. Examples of decimal literal follow:

```
99.999
0.1
1.0
```

2.4.3.2 Integer Literals

Integer literals are used to write integral values.

IntegerLiteral:

   DecimalDigits

Integer literals default to the smallest precision type that can contain the value, starting with `Integer32`.

Examples of integer literal follow:

```
0
123
99999999999999999999999999999999
```

2.4.3.3 Scientific Literals

Scientific literals are used to write values floating-point or inexact numbers.

ScientificLiteral:

   DecimalLiteral **e** *Sign$_{opt}$ DecimalDigit DecimalDigits$_{opt}$*

   DecimalLiteral **E** *Sign$_{opt}$ DecimalDigit DecimalDigits$_{opt}$*

Sign: one of

   +   –

Scientific literals default to the smallest precision type that can contain the value, starting with Double.

Examples of scientific literal follow:

```
.31416e+1
9.9999e-1
0.0E0
```

2.4.3.4 Date Literals

Date literals are used to write a date independent of a specific time of day.

DateLiteral:

$Sign_{opt}$ *DateYear* – *DateMonth* – *DateDay*

The tokens of a *DateLiteral* must not have white space.

DateDay: one of

```
01   02   03   04   05   06   07   08   09   10   11   12   13   14   15   16   17
18   19   20   21   22   23   24   25   26   27   28   29   30   31
```

DateMonth: one of

```
01   02   03   04   05   06   07   08   09   10   11   12
```

DateYear:

DecimalDigit DecimalDigit DecimalDigit DecimalDigit

The type of a *DateLiteral* is Date.

- 0001-01-01 is the representation of January1[st], 1 AD.
- There is no year 0, therefore '0000' is not a valid Date Time.
- -0001 is the representation of January1[st], 1 BC.

Examples of date literal follow:

```
0001-01-01
2008-08-14
-1184-03-01
```

2.4.3.5 DateTime Literals

DateTime literals are used to write a time of day on a specific date independent of time zone.

DateTimeLiteral:

   DateLiteral T *TimeLiteral*

The type of a DateTime literal is `DateTime`.
   Example of date time literal follow:

```
2008-08-14T13:13:00
0001-01-01T00:00:00
2005-05-19T20:05:00
```

2.4.3.6 Time Literals

TimeLiteral:

   TimeHourMinute : *TimeSecond*

TimeHourMinute:

   TimeHour : *TimeMinute*

TimeHour: one of

00	01	02	03	04	05	06	07	08	09	10	11
12	13	14	15	16	17	18	19	20	21	22	23

TimeMinute:

   0   DecimalDigit

   1   DecimalDigit

   2   DecimalDigit

   3   DecimalDigit

   4   DecimalDigit

   5   DecimalDigit

TimeSecond:

   0 *DecimalDigit TimeSecondDecimalPart$_{opt}$*

   1 *DecimalDigit TimeSecondDecimalPart$_{opt}$*

   2 *DecimalDigit TimeSecondDecimalPart$_{opt}$*

   3 *DecimalDigit TimeSecondDecimalPart$_{opt}$*

   4 *DecimalDigit TimeSecondDecimalPart$_{opt}$*

   5 *DecimalDigit TimeSecondDecimalPart$_{opt}$*

   60 *TimeSecondDecimalPart$_{opt}$*

TimeSecondDecimalPart:

   . *DecimalDigits*

Examples of time literal follow:

```
11:30:00
01:01:01.111
13:13:00
```

2.4.3.7 Character Literals

A character literal represents a single character, for example `'a'`.

CharacterLiteral:

   ' *Character* '

Character:

   CharacterSimple

   CharacterEscapeHex

   CharacterEscapeSimple

   CharacterEscapeUnicode

Characters:

   Character

   Characters Character

CharacterEscapeHex:

   CharacterEscapeHexPrefix HexDigit

   CharacterEscapeHexPrefix HexDigit HexDigit

   CharacterEscapeHexPrefix HexDigit HexDigit HexDigit

   CharacterEscapeHexPrefix HexDigit HexDigit HexDigit HexDigit

   CharacterEscapeHexPrefix: one of

```
\x   \X
```

CharacterEscapeSimple:

   \   *CharacterEscapeSimpleCharacter*

CharacterEscapeSimpleCharacter: one of

```
'   "   \   0   a   b   f   n   r   t   v
```

CharacterEscapeUnicode:

   \u   *HexDigit HexDigit HexDigit HexDigit*

   \U   *HexDigit HexDigit HexDigit HexDigit HexDigit HexDigit HexDigit HexDigit*

CharacterSimple: none of

   U+0027 *// Single Quote*

   U+005C *// Backslash*

   NewLineCharacter

A hexadecimal escape sequence represents a single Unicode character, with the value formed by the hexadecimal number following the prefix.

If the value represented by a character literal is greater than U+FFFF, a compile-time error occurs.

A Unicode character escape sequence in a character literal must be in the range U+0000 to U+FFFF.

A simple escape sequence represents a Unicode character encoding, as described in the following table.

Escape Sequence	Character Name	Unicode Encoding
\'	Single quote	0x0027
\"	Double quote	0x0022
\\	Backslash	0x005C
\0	Null	0x0000
\a	Alert	0x0007
\b	Backspace	0x0008
\f	Form feed	0x000C
\n	New line	0x000A
\r	Carriage return	0x000D
\t	Horizontal tab	0x0009
\v	Vertical tab	0x000B

Since M uses a 16-bit encoding of Unicode code points in `Character` and `Text` values, a Unicode character in the range U+10000 to U+10FFFF is not permitted in a `Character` literal and is represented using a Unicode surrogate pair in a `Text` literal. Unicode characters with code points above 0x10FFFF are not supported.

Multiple translations are not performed. For instance, the `Text` literal \u005Cu005C is equivalent to \u005C rather than \. The Unicode value U+005C is the character \.

The type of a `Character` literal is `Character`.

Examples of a character `literal` follow:

```
'a'
'\u2323'
'\x2323'
```

2.4.3.8 Text Literals

M supports two forms of `Text` literals: regular `Text` literals and verbatim `Text` literals.

A regular `Text` literal consists of zero or more characters enclosed in double quotes, as in `"hello"` and may include both simple escape sequences (such as \t for the tab character), and hexadecimal and Unicode escape sequences.

A verbatim `Text` literal consists of an @ character followed by a double-quote character, zero or more characters, and a closing double-quote character. A simple example is @`"hello"`. In a verbatim `Text` literal, the characters between the delimiters are interpreted exactly as they occur in the compilation unit, the only exception being a *QuoteEscapeSequence*. In particular, simple escape sequences, and hexadecimal and Unicode escape sequences are not processed in verbatim `Text` literals. A verbatim `Text` literal may span multiple lines.

TextLiteral:

    " *TextCharacters*$_{opt}$ "

    @ " *TextVerbatimCharacters*$_{opt}$ "

TextCharacter:

  TextSimple

  CharacterEscapeHex

CharacterEscapeSimple

CharacterEscapeUnicode

TextCharacters:

   TextCharacter

   TextCharacters TextCharacter

TextSimple: none of

   "

   \

   NewLineCharacter

TextVerbatimCharacter:

   none of "

   TextVerbatimCharacterEscape

TextVerbatimCharacterEscape:

   " "

TextVerbatimCharacters:

   TextVerbatimCharacter+ ;

   TextVerbatimCharacters TextVerbatimCharacter

The type of a Text literal is `Text`.
   Examples of text literal follow:

```
"Hello World"
@"""Hello World"""
"\u2323"
```

2.4.3.9 Logical Literals

Logical literals are used to write logical values.

LogicalLiteral: one of

   true   false

The type of a Logical literal is `Logical`.

Examples of logical literal:

```
true
false
```

2.4.3.10 Binary and Byte Literals

Binary literals are used to write binary and byte values.

BinaryLiteral:

    0x *HexDigits*$_{opt}$

    0X *HexDigits*$_{opt}$

HexDigit: one of

    0   1   2   3   4   5   6   7   8   9   0   a   b   c   d   e   f   A   B   C   M   E   F

HexDigits:

    HexDigit HexDigit

    HexDigits HexDigit HexDigit

The type of a Binary literal with two digits defaults to `Binary`. Binary literals with two digits default to `Byte`.

    Examples of byte literal follow:

```
0x00
0XFF
0x01
```

Examples of binary literal follow:

```
0x
0x0000000000000000000000000000000000000000000
0x1234
```

2.4.3.11 Null Literal

The null literal is equal to no other value.

NullLiteral:

```
null
```

The type of a null literal is `Null`.
An example of the null literal follows:

```
null
```

2.4.3.12 Guid Literals

GuidLiteral:

```
#[ X X X X X X X X - X X X X - X X X X - X X X X - X X X X X X X X X X X X ]
```

X:

HexDigit

The type of a Guid literal is `Guid`.
Examples of Guid literal follows:

```
#[a0ee7e0f-c6ac-4c63-b57f-816a5259595a]
#[7fbc28ba-8205-45ca-983e-ece117f7a776]
#[a05e63ca-25de-43a6-bf70-0bc04d40a000]
```

2.4.4 Operators and Punctuators

There are several kinds of operators and punctuators. Operators are used in expressions to describe operations involving one or more operands. For example, the expression a + b uses the + operator to add the two operands a and b. Punctuators are for grouping and separating.

OperatorOrPunctuator: one of

```
[ ] ( ) . , : ; ? = < > <= >= == != + - ° / % & | ! && || ~ << >> { } # .. @ ' " ??
```

2.5 Pre-processing Directives

Pre-processing directives provide the ability to conditionally skip sections of source files, to report error and warning conditions, and to delineate distinct regions of source code as a separate pre-processing step.

PPDirective:

   PPDeclaration

   PPConditional

   PPDiagnostic

   PPRegion

The following pre-processing directives are available:

- `#define` and `#undef`, which are used to define and undefine, respectively, conditional compilation symbols.
- `#if`, `#else`, and `#endif`, which are used to conditionally skip sections of source code.

A pre-processing directive always occupies a separate line of source code and always begins with a `#` character and a pre-processing directive name. White space may occur before the `#` character and between the `#` character and the directive name.

A source line containing a `#define`, `#undef`, `#if`, `#else`, or `#endif` directive may end with a single-line comment. Delimited comments (the `/* */` style of comments) are not permitted on source lines containing pre-processing directives.

Pre-processing directives are neither tokens nor part of the syntactic grammar of M. However, pre-processing directives can be used to include or exclude sequences of tokens and can in that way affect the meaning of an M program. For example, after pre-processing the source text:

```
#define A
#undef B
type C
{
#if A
    F {}
#else
```

```
    G {}
#endif
#if B
    H {}
#else
    I {}
#endif
}
```

results in the exact same sequence of tokens as the source text:

```
type C
{
    F {}
    I {}
}
```

Thus, whereas lexically, the two programs are quite different, syntactically, they are identical.

2.5.1 Conditional Compilation Symbols

The conditional compilation functionality provided by the `#if`, `#else`, and `#endif` directives is controlled through pre-processing expressions and conditional compilation symbols.

ConditionalSymbol:

> Any *IdentifierOrKeyword* `except true or false`

A conditional compilation symbol has two possible states: defined or undefined. At the beginning of the lexical processing of a source file, a conditional compilation symbol is undefined unless it has been explicitly defined by an external mechanism (such as a command-line compiler option). When a `#define` directive is processed, the conditional compilation symbol named in that directive becomes defined in that source file. The symbol remains defined until an `#undef` directive for that same symbol is processed, or until the end of the source file is reached. An implication of this is that `#define` and `#undef` directives in one source file have no effect on other source files in the same program.

When referenced in a pre-processing expression, a defined conditional compilation symbol has the Logical value `true`, and an undefined conditional compilation symbol has the Logical value `false`. There is no requirement that conditional compilation symbols be explicitly declared before they are referenced in pre-processing expressions. Instead, undeclared symbols are simply undefined and thus have the value `false`.

Conditional compilation symbols can only be referenced in `#define` and `#undef` directives and in pre-processing expressions.

2.5.2 Pre-processing Expressions

Pre-processing expressions can occur in `#if` directives. The operators `!`, `==`, `!=`, `&&`, and `||` are permitted in pre-processing expressions, and parentheses may be used for grouping.

PPExpression:

   Whitespace$_{opt}$ PPOrExpression   Whitespace$_{opt}$

OrExpression:

   PPAndExpression

   PPOrExpression   Whitespace$_{opt}$ || Whitespace$_{opt}$ PPAndExpression

PPAndExpression:

   PPEqualityExpression

   PPAndExpression Whitespace$_{opt}$ && Whitespace$_{opt}$ PPEqualityExpression

PPEqualityExpression:

   PPUnaryExpression

   PPEqualityExpression   Whitespace$_{opt}$ == Whitespace$_{opt}$ PPUnaryExpression

   PPEqualityExpression   Whitespace$_{opt}$!= Whitespace$_{opt}$ PPUnaryExpression

PPUnaryExpression:

   PPPrimaryExpression

   ! Whitespace$_{opt}$ PPUnaryExpression

PPPrimaryExpression:

   true

   false

   ConditionalSymbol

   (Whitespace$_{opt}$ PPExpression Whitespace$_{opt}$)

When referenced in a pre-processing expression, a defined conditional compilation symbol has the Logical value `true`, and an undefined conditional compilation symbol has the Logical value `false`.

Evaluation of a pre-processing expression always yields a Logical value. The rules of evaluation for a pre-processing expression are the same as those for a constant expression, except that the only user-defined entities that can be referenced are conditional compilation symbols.

2.5.3 Declaration Directives

The declaration directives are used to define or undefine conditional compilation symbols.

PPDeclaration:

    Whitespace$_{opt}$ # *Whitespace$_{opt}$* define *Whitespace* *ConditionalSymbol* *PPNewLine*

    Whitespace$_{opt}$ # *Whitespace$_{opt}$* undef *Whitespace* *ConditionalSymbol* *PPNewLine*

PPNewLine:

    Whitespace$_{opt}$ *SingleLineComment$_{opt}$* *NewLine*

The processing of a `#define` directive causes the given conditional compilation symbol to become defined, starting with the source line that follows the directive. Likewise, the processing of an `#undef` directive causes the given conditional compilation symbol to become undefined, starting with the source line that follows the directive.

A `#define` may define a conditional compilation symbol that is already defined, without there being any intervening `#undef` for that symbol. The following example defines a conditional compilation symbol A and then defines it again.

```
#define A
#define A
```

A `#undef` may "undefine" a conditional compilation symbol that is not defined. The example below defines a conditional compilation symbol A and then undefines it twice; although the second `#undef` has no effect, it is still valid.

```
#define A
#undef A
#undef A
```

2.5.4 Conditional Compilation Directives

The conditional compilation directives are used to conditionally include or exclude portions of a source file.

PPConditional:

    PPIfSection   *PPElseSection*$_{opt}$ *PPEndif*

PPIfSection:

    Whitespace$_{opt}$ #   *Whitespace*$_{opt}$ `if`   *Whitespace*   *PPExpression*   *PPNewLine*   *ConditionalSection*$_{opt}$

PPElseSection:

    Whitespace$_{opt}$ #   *Whitespace*$_{opt}$ `else`   *PPNewLine*   *ConditionalSection*$_{opt}$

PPEndif:

    Whitespace$_{opt}$ #   *Whitespace*$_{opt}$ `endif`   *PPNewLine*

ConditionalSection:

    InputSection

    SkippedSection

SkippedSection:

    SkippedSectionPart

    SkippedSection   *SkippedSectionPart*

SkippedSectionPart:

    SkippedCharacters$_{opt}$ *NewLine*

    PPDirective

SkippedCharacters:

    Whitespace$_{opt}$ *NotNumberSign*   *InputCharacters*$_{opt}$

NotNumberSign:

      Any   *InputCharacter*   except   #

As indicated by the syntax, conditional compilation directives must be written as sets consisting of, in order, an `#if` directive, zero or one `#else` directive, and an `#endif` directive. Between the directives are conditional sections of source code. Each section is controlled by the immediately preceding directive. A conditional section may itself contain nested conditional compilation directives provided these directives form complete sets.

A *PPConditional* selects at most one of the contained *ConditionalSections* for normal lexical processing:

- The *PPExpressions* of the `#if` directives are evaluated in order until one yields `true`. If an expression yields `true`, the *ConditionalSection* of the corresponding directive is selected.
- If all *PPExpressions* yield `false`, and if an `#else` directive is present, the *ConditionalSection* of the `#else` directive is selected.
- Otherwise, no *ConditionalSection* is selected.

The selected *ConditionalSection*, if any, is processed as a normal *InputSection*: The source code contained in the section must adhere to the lexical grammar; tokens are generated from the source code in the section; and pre-processing directives in the section have the prescribed effects.

The remaining *ConditionalSections*, if any, are processed as *SkippedSections*: Except for pre-processing directives, the source code in the section need not adhere to the lexical grammar; no tokens are generated from the source code in the section; and pre-processing directives in the section must be lexically correct but are not otherwise processed. Within a *ConditionalSection* that is being processed as a *SkippedSection*, any nested *ConditionalSections* (contained in nested `#if`...`#endif` and `#region`...`#endregion` constructs) are also processed as *SkippedSections*.

Except for pre-processing directives, skipped source code is not subject to lexical analysis. For example, the following is valid despite the unterminated comment in the `#else` section:

```
#define Debug          // Debugging on
type Purchase
{
    ExtendedPrice {
#if Debug
        Price * Quantity;
#else
        /* Unterminated comment!
#endif
    }
}
```

Note that pre-processing directives are required to be lexically correct even in skipped sections of source code.

Pre-processing directives are not processed when they appear inside multiline input elements. For example, the program:

```
type Hello
{
    World =  @"hello,
#if Debug
        world
#else
        Nebraska
#endif
        ";
    }
}
```

assigns the world field the value:

```
hello,
#if Debug
        world
#else
        Nebraska
#endif
```

In peculiar cases, the set of pre-processing directives that is processed might depend on the evaluation of the *PPExpression*. The example:

```
#if X
    /*
#else
    /* */ type Q { }
#endif
```

always produces the same token stream (`type Q { }`), regardless of whether x is defined. If x is defined, the only processed directives are `#if` and `#endif`, due to the multiline comment. If x is undefined, then three directives (`#if`, `#else`, `#endif`) are part of the directive set.

CHAPTER 3

TYPES

The types of the M lansguage are divided into two main categories: intrinsic types and derived types. An intrinsic type is a type that cannot be defined using M language constructs but rather is defined entirely in the M Language Specification. An *intrinsic* type (for example, Number, Entity, Collection) may name a supertype as part of its specification. Values are an instance of exactly one intrinsic type, and conform to the specification of that one intrinsic type and all of its supertypes.

A *derived* type (for example, Integer32, Person, Cars) is a type whose definition is constructed in M source text using the type constructors that are provided in the language. A derived type is defined as a constraint over another type, which creates an explicit subtyping relationship. Values conform to any number of derived types simply by virtue of satisfying the derived type's constraint. There is no explicit affiliation between a value and a derived type—rather a given value that conforms to a derived type's constraint may be interpreted as that type or any other derived type using type *ascription*.

3.1 Type Declaration

M offers a broad range of options in defining types. Any expression that returns a collection can be declared as a type. The type predicates for entities and collections are expressions and fit this form. A type declaration may explicitly enumerate its members or be composed of other types.

The syntax for a type declaration follows:

TypeDeclaration:

    type *Identifier* ;

    type *Identifier InitializationExpression* ;_{opt}

    type *Identifier EntityTypeExpression* ;_{opt}

    type *Identifier EntityTypeExpression* where *WhereExpressions* ;

```
type Identifier : Expression ;

type Identifier : TypeReferences ;

type Identifier : TypeReferences EntityTypeExpression ; opt

type Identifier : TypeReferences EntityTypeExpression where WhereExpressions ;
```

The *Identifier* in a type declaration introduces a new symbol into the module level scope:

TypeReference:

  QualifiedIdentifier

TypeReferences:

  TypeReference

  TypeReferences , TypeReference

The *QualifiedIdentifier* in *TypeReference* must either refer to a type declared in the current module or to an exported type from a module that is imported by the current module.

The declaration:

```
type SomeNewType;
```

declares a new type SomeNewType with no constraints. Any value satisfies this type.

The following example explicitly enumerates the values of type PrimaryColors and uses it in the *EntityExpression* that defines the type Car:

```
type\ PrimaryColors {"Red", "Blue", "Yellow"}

type Car {
    Make : Text;
    Model : Text;
    Color : PrimaryColors;
}
```

These common cases do not require a colon between the declaration name and the definition.

Type declarations can be built up from expressions that return collections. The type PrimaryColors above could be constructed from singleton sets.

```
type PrimaryColors2 : {"Red"} | {"Blue"} | {"Yellow"}
```

Since the expression `{"Red"}` | `{"Blue"}` | `{"Yellow"}` == `{"Red"`, `"Blue"`, `"Yellow"}` the two declarations are equivalent.

However an expression which does not return a collection is not a semantically valid type.

```
type NonSense : 1 + 1;
```

is a syntactically valid declaration but not useful as a type since no value of x would ever satisfy the following expression because 2 is not a collection:

```
X in 2
```

Entity types may be composed as well. Consider the following two distinct types:

```
type Vehicle {
    Owner : Text;
    Registration : Text;
}
```

```
type HasWheels {
    Wheels : Integer32;
}
```

The type `Vehicle` requires that instances have `Owner` and `Registration` fields. The type `HasWheels` requires instances have a `Wheels` field. These two types can be combined into a new type `Car` that requires `Owner`, `Registration`, and `Wheels` fields.

```
type Car : Vehicle & HasWheels;
```

In this usage, ampersand requires that `Car` meet all the requirements of both arguments.

This definition of `Car` can be further restricted since cars have four wheels. Such restrictions can be specified with a constraint (Section 5.16.1):

```
type Car2 : Vehicle & HasWheels where value.Wheels == 4;
```

It is common to extend types with additional fields and restrict values. M provides the following syntax to simplify this case:

```
type Car3 : Vehicle {
    Wheels : Integer32;
} where value.Wheels == 4;
```

3.2 This

A type declaration creates a new scope containing the symbol `this` which refers to instances of the constructed type. It is used to explicitly refer to instances of the created type and their members.

In the following example, the member `Age` is masked by a formal parameter, necessitating the use of the `this` symbol:

```
type Adult {
    // this is in scope
    Name : Text;
    Age : Integer32;
    Older(Age:Integer32) : Logical {
        this.Age > Age;
    }
}
```

3.3 Subtyping

M is a structurally typed language rather than a nominally typed language like C++ or C#. A structural type is a specification for a set of values. Two types are equivalent if the exact same collection of values conforms to both regardless of the name of the types.

It is not required that a type be named to be used. A type expression is allowed wherever a type reference is required. Types in M are simply expressions that return collections.

If every value that conforms to type A also conforms to type B, we say that A is a *subtype* of B (and that B is a *supertype* of A). Subtyping is transitive, that is, if A is a subtype of B and B is a subtype of C, then A is a subtype of C (and C is a supertype of A). Subtyping is reflexive, that is, A is a (vacuous) subtype of A (and A is a supertype of A).

3.4 Operators

Types are considered collections of all values that satisfy the type predicate. For that reason, any operation on a collection (Section 3.7.2) can be applied to a type, and a type can be manipulated with expressions like any other collection value.

The relational operators (`<`, `>`, `<=`, `>=`, `==`, `!=`) compare the value spaces of two types and return a `Logical` value. For example, the operator `<=` on types computes the subtype relation:

```
(Car <= Vehicle) == true
(Car <= HasWheels) == true
(Car <= Colors) == false
```

The `where` constraint restricts the value space of a type to those elements satisfying the right operand's logical expression.

The following binary operations take `Collection` as a left operand.

Operator	Right Operand	Return
`&`, `|`	Collection	Collection

The union and intersection operators (`|`, `&`) operate on the type's value spaces. Intersection, `&`, can be thought of as specialization, restriction, or subtyping. Union, `|`, can be thought of as generalization or inducing a supertype.

The following postfix operators take types as a left operand.

Operator	Return
`?`	Type
`+` `*`	Type
`#m..n`	Type

`?` is a postfix operator that adds `null` to the value space of its operand. `T?` is equivalent to

```
T | { null }
```

The multiplicities lift a type to a collection of that type with the appropriate cardinality. For example:

```
Date*        // A collection of any number of dates
Person+      // A collection of one or more people
Wheel#2..4   // A collection of two to four wheels
```

3.5 Intrinsic Types

The following table lists the intrinsic types that are defined as part of the M Language Specification.

Type	Super Type	Description
Any		All values
General	Any	All simple values
Number	General	Any numeric value
Decimal	Number	A fixed-point or exact number
Integer	Decimal	A signed, integral value
Unsigned	Integer	An unsigned, integral value
Scientific	Number	A floating-point or exact number
Date	General	A calendar date
DateTime	General	A calendar date and time of day
Time	General	A time of day and time zone
Text	General	A sequence of Characters
Character	General	A single Unicode character of text
Logical	General	A logical flag
Binary	General	A sequence of binary octets
Guid	General	A globally unique identifier
Byte	General	A single binary octet
Collection	Any	An unordered group of (potentially duplicate) values
Entity	Any	A collection of labeled values
Null	Any	Contains the single value `null`

3.5.1 Any

All values are members of this type.

The following binary operations take `Any` as a left operand.

Operator	Right Operand	Return
in	Collection	Logical

The `in` operator returns true if some member of the right operand is equal (`==`) to the left operand.

3.5.2 General

All values that are not members of Entity or Collection (or null) are members of this type. It has no additional operators beyond those defined on Any.

3.5.3 Number

Number is an abstract type with four abstract subtypes enumerated in the following table. Each of these subtypes is further refined to a concrete type with a precision. A concrete type of a smaller precision may always be converted to the same type of a larger precision. Converting from a larger precision to a smaller precision tests for overflow at runtime.

The arithmetic operations (`+`, `-`, `*`, `/`, `%`) defined above are specialized to return the most specific type of its operands (for example, `Integer8 + Integer8` returns `Integer8`, `Decimal9 + Decimal38` returns `Decimal38`).

Abstract Type	Concrete Type
Integer	Integer8
	Integer16
	Integer32
	Integer64

Abstract Type	Concrete Type
Unsigned	Unsigned8
	Unsigned16
	Unsigned32
	Unsigned64
Decimal	Decimal9
	Decimal19
	Decimal28
	Decimal38
Scientific	Single
	Double

3.5.3.1 Operators

The following unary operations take `Number` as a right operand.

Operator	Return
+, -	Number

The following binary operations take `Number` as a left operand.

Operator	Right Operand	Return
+, -	Number	Number
*, /, %	Number	Number
>, <, <=, >=, ==, !=	Number	Logical

The following operations may cause underflow and overflow errors:

- The predefined unary - operator
- The predefined +, -, *, and / binary operators
- Explicit numeric conversions from one Number type to another

The following operations may cause a divide-by-zero error:

- The predefined / and % binary operators

3.5.3.2 AutoNumber

Unique numbers can be generated with the AutoNumber computed value. This is a special form for ensuring unique identities. Consider the following example:

```
type Person {
    Id : Integer32 = AutoNumber();
    Name : Text;
    Age : Integer32;
    Spouse : Person;
} where identity Id;

People : Person*;
```

Each instance of `Person` will receive an `Id` value that is unique for each extent that contains `Person` instances.

AutoNumber has a number of restrictions. The default value should not be overridden, and AutoNumber may only be used on identity fields.

3.5.4 Text

The representation of text is implementation-dependent.

The following postfix operator takes `Text` as a left operand.

Operator	Return
#	Unsigned

The postfix # operator returns the count of characters in a `Text` string.

The following binary operations take `Text` as a left operand.

Operator	Right Operand	Return
+	Text	Text
>, <, <=, >=, ==, !=	Text	Logical

The binary + operator concatenates two Text strings.

The relational operators perform a lexicographic comparison on the Text strings and return a Logical value.

3.5.4.1 Members

The following members are defined on Text.

```
Count() : Unsigned;
Like(pattern : Text) : Logical;
PatternIndex(pattern : Text) : Integer;
```

Count provides the number of characters in the text.

Like returns true if the input is matched by the pattern.

PatternIndex returns the starting position of the pattern in the text or -1 if the pattern is not found.

The pattern is of the following form:

Pattern

   PatternElement

   Pattern PatternElement

PatternElement

   NormalCharacter

   -

   %

   [*NormalCharacter - NormalCharacter*]

   [^ *NormalCharacter - NormalCharacter*]

Dash matches any single character. Percent matches zero or more characters. A character range matches any single character in the range. And an excluded character range matches any character not in the range.

3.5.4.2 Declaration

The # qualifier is overloaded on Text declarations to constrain the length of the text field. The expression

```
Text#N;
```

is equivalent to

```
Text where value.Count <= N;
```

3.5.5 Character

The following binary operations take `Character` as a left operand.

Operator	Right Operand	Return
>, <, <=, >=, ==, !=	Character	Logical

The relational operators perform a comparison and return a `Logical` value.

3.5.6 Logical

The following unary operator takes `Logical` as an operand.

Operator	Return
!	Logical

The following binary operations take `Logical` as a left operand.

Operator	Right Operand	Return
&&, ||	Logical	Logical
==, !=	Logical	Logical

The following ternary operator takes `Logical` as a right operand.

Operator	Middle Operand	Left Operand	Return
? :	Any	Any	Any

3.5.7 Binary and Byte

The following unary operator takes `Binary` as a right operand.

Operator	Return
~	Binary

The ~ operator computes the bitwise negation of its operand.

The following binary operations take `Binary` as a left operand.

Operator	Right Operand	Return
<<, >>	Integer	Binary
==, !=	Logical	Logical
&, |, ^	Binary	Binary

The left shift operator << discards n high-order bits, shifts remaining bits left, and zeros the low-order empty bit positions. Similarly, the right shift operator >> discards n low-order bits, shifts remaining bits right, and zeros the high-order empty bit positions. The result of left shift and right shift has the same length as the left operand.

The bitwise and, bitwise exclusive or, and bitwise or operators implicitly convert their operands to the same length. The smaller operand is padded with zeros on the left.

The precedence of the bitwise and, or, and exclusive or is lower than it is in many other languages.

3.5.8 Guid

The following binary operations take Guid as a left operand.

Operator	Right Operand	Return
==, !=	Guid	Logical

Guids are created with the system-defined NewGuid computed value.

```
NewGuid() : Guid;
```

3.5.9 Date

The following binary operations take Date as a left operand.

Operator	Right Operand	Return
+	Time	DateTime
>, <, <=, >=, ==, !=	Date	Logical

3.5.10 DateTime

The following binary operations take DateTime as a left operand.

Operator	Right Operand	Return
>, <, <=, >=, ==, !=	DateTime	Logical

3.5.11 Time

The following binary operations take Time as a left operand.

Operator	Right Operand	Return
+	Date	DateTime
>, <, <=, >=, ==, !=	Time	Logical

3.6 Entity

An *EntityTypeExpression* specifies the members for a set of entity values (commonly referred to as entities). Those members can be either *fields* or *computed values*.

Entity types are distinct from extents. The definition of an entity type does not imply allocation of storage. Storage is allocated when an extent of entity type is declared within a module.

Entities may have identity. The fields of an entity can be assigned default values, and the values can be constrained with expressions. The names of all fields must be distinct.

3.6.1 Declaration

The following syntax defines a collection of all possible instances that satisfy the structure and constraint.

EntityTypeExpression:

    { *EntityMemberDeclarations* }

EntityMemberDeclarations:

    EntityMemberDeclaration

    EntityMemberDeclarations EntityMemberDeclaration

EntityMemberDeclaration:

    FieldDeclaration

    ComputedValueDeclaration

Entity declarations share *FieldDeclaration* and *ComputedValueDeclaration* with module. It is an error to declare two *FieldDeclarations* with different default values.

3.6.2 Identity

The `identity` constraint controls the representation of identity. If it is specified, the selected fields are used to represent the identity. If no `identity` constraint is specified, the entity cannot be referenced. Placing the identity constraint on a field makes that field initialize only. It cannot be updated.

The `identity` constraint may be specified either on entity declarations or on extent declarations, not both. The `identity` constraint requires that the elements in the constraint are unique within each extent (not across extents) as with the `unique` constraint. An identity declaration on a derived type supersedes that of any types it derives from. As a result, there can be only one identity constraint on an entity or an extent.

Consider the following example:

```
type Container {
    Id : Integer32;
    Capacity: Integer32;
} where identity Id;

CoffeeCups : Container* { {Id = 1, Capacity = 12} }
WaterBottles : Container* { {Id = 1, Capacity = 12} }

EqualityTest() {
    from c in CoffeeCups
    from w in WaterBottles
    where c == w
    select "Never"
}
```

It is legal for the two extents to contain instances whose `Id` fields are equal. Having the same `Id` field does not equate the instances. The computed value `EqualityTest` will always return the empty collection because identity is relative to an extent.

An implementation of M may restrict the types of fields used to form identity.

3.6.3 Operators

The following binary operations take `Entity` as a left operand.

Operator	Right Operand	Return
==, !=	Entity	Logical

The equality operations on entities compare identity (shallow equal). == returns true if both operands refer to an instance with the same identity in the same collection.

3.6.4 Members

The following member is defined on all entities:

```
FieldNames() : Text*;
```

FieldNames returns the string names of each label in an instance. This member is not affected by ascription and does not return names of computed values or missing default values.

3.6.5 Indexer

Entities have a default indexer that accepts field name as text and returns the value of the field if present or null:

```
{Name = "Bob"}("Name")  == "Bob"
{Name = "Bob"}("Age")   == null
```

The indexer accesses the underlying instance data without interpretation by the type. This allows the indexer to access field values that may be hidden by a computed value. Consider

```
type Hider {
    Name() : Text { "Hides instance values" };
}
```

Given the preceding declaration, the following two expressions would evaluate to true.

```
({Name = "Underlying value"} : Hider).Name == "Hides instance values"
({Name = "Underlying value"} : Hider)("Name") == "Underlying value"
```

3.6.6 Ascription

An entity defines a constraint over a set of values. An entity type can be ascribed to any value that satisfies its constraint. Ascribing an entity type allows the computed values defined in the entity to be applied to the value.

Consider the following two entities and two instances. (The square root [SQRT] and absolute value [ABS] functions must be provided by a library; they are not intrinsic.)

```
type PointOnPlane {
    X : Single;
    Y : Single;
    DistanceFromOrigin : Single { SQRT(X * X + Y * Y) }
}

type PointOnLine {
    X : Single;
    Y : Single;
    DistanceFromOrigin : Single { ABS(X) * SQRT(2) }
} where X == Y;

Point1 = {X=1, Y=1};
Point2 = {X=0, Y=1};
```

Both entities define fields x and y and a computed value DistanceFromOrigin although the implementation of the computed value differs. The first entity, PointOnPlane, allows any X,Y combination—the entire X,Y plane. The second entity, PointOnLine, has a constraint that restricts the values that can be members of the type.

Point1 is a member of both PointOnPlane and PointOnLine. Both declarations of DistanceFromOrigin are valid and yield the same result.

Point2 can be ascribed PointOnPlane but not of PointOnLine since the constraint X == Y is not satisfied. This prevents the alternative declaration of DistanceFromOrigin from producing an incorrect result.

3.7 Collections

Collections are unordered and may contain elements that are equal. M provides operators to construct strongly typed collections and in some cases defined next escalates members on elements to members on the collection.

3.7.1 Declaration

New collection types are defined by a type constructor and a multiplicity (`+`, `*`, `#m..n`).

Type Expression	Equivalent Type
TypeReference `*`	`Collection where item in` *TypeReference*
TypeReference `+`	`Collection where item in` *TypeReference* `&& value.Count >= 1`
TypeReference `#` *Integer*	`Collection where ElementType ==` *TypeReference* `&& value.Count == Integer`

TypeReference `#` *Low* .. *High*	`Collection where ElementType ==` *TypeReference*
	`&& value.Count >= Low`
	`&& value.Count <= High`

TypeReference `#` *Integer* ..	`Collection where ElementType ==` *TypeReference* `&& value.Count >= Integer`

The default value for a collection type is the empty collection, written `{}`. The one-to-many multiplicity constraint forbids an empty collection so must have at least one member on initialization.

3.7.2 Operators

The following postfix unary operator takes `Collection` as a left operand.

Operator	Return
`#`	`Unsigned`

The following binary operations take `Collection` as a left operand.

Operator	Right Operand	Return
>, <, <=, >=, ==, !=	Collection	Logical
where	Logical	Collection
select	Any	Collection
&, |, \	Collection	Collection

For the operators that return a collection, the inferred element type of the resulting collection is the most specific type that the elements of both operands may be converted to.

3.7.3 Members

The following members are defined on all collections:

```
Choose() : Any;
Count() : Unsigned;
Distinct() : Collection;
```

Choose picks an arbitrary element from a collection. The return type is the element type. Count returns the total number of elements in a collection. The return type is a Number. Distinct removes all duplicates in a collection. The return type is the same as the collection.

The following members are defined on collections of type Logical*:

```
All() : Logical;
Exists() : Logical;
```

All returns false if false is an element of the collection and true otherwise. Exists returns true if true is an element of the collection and false otherwise.

The following members are defined on collections that are subtypes of Number*:

```
Average() : Scientific;
Maximum() : Number;
Minimum() : Number;
Sum() : Number;
```

Maximum, Minimum, and Sum are specialized to return the element type of the collection.

3.7.4 Indexers

A collection may be accessed using language generated indexers of two kinds, selectors and projectors. A selector extracts members of a collection with a member that matches a value. A projector extracts all values of a field from a collection. Both of these operations can be accomplished with query expressions; however, this notation is more compact.

3.7.4.1 Selectors

The compiler will generate indexers for all fields of Person for Person*.
Consider the following example:

```
type Person {
    Id : Integer64 = AutoNumber();
    Name : Text;
    HairColor : Text;
} where identity Id, unique Name;

People : Person* {
    {Name = "Mary", HairColor = "Brown"},
    {Name = "John", HairColor = "Brown"},
    {Name = "Fritz", HairColor = "Blue"}
};
```

Consider the following expressions:

```
People.Name("Mary")
```

evaluates to:

```
{{Name = "Mary", HairColor = "Brown" }}
```

```
People.Name("Bill")
```

evaluates to:

```
{}
```

```
People.HairColor("Brown")
```

evaluates to:

```
{
    {Name = "Mary", HairColor = "Brown" },
    {Name = "John", HairColor = "Brown"}
}
```

```
// Assuming the Fritz record was assigned the Id 123
People.Id(123)
```

evaluates to:

```
{{Name = "Fritz", HairColor = "Blue"}}
```

The expression:

```
Collection.MemberField(Expression)
```

is equivalent to:

```
from c in Collection
where c.MemberField == Expression
select c
```

The identity auto indexer is special in that it is also an indexer directly on the collection, so the following expression is legal:

```
People(123) == {{Name = "Fritz", HairColor = "Blue"}}
```

If the designer chose a different representation for identity, it would be the default indexer as shown in the following variant of the preceding example:

```
type Person Scdt1
{
    Name : Text;
    HairColor : Text;
} where identity Name;

People("Mary") == {{Name = "Mary", HairColor = "Brown" }}
```

The expression:

```
Collection (Expression)
```

is equivalent to:

```
from c in Collection
where c.Identity == Expression
select c
```

3.7.4.2 Projectors

Projectors return all the values of a member of a collection.

Again, consider the following example:

```
type Person {
    Id : Integer64 = AutoNumber();
    Name : Text;
    HairColor : Text;
} where identity Id, unique Name;

People : Person* {
    {Name = "Mary", HairColor = "Brown"},
    {Name = "John", HairColor = "Brown"},
    {Name = "Fritz", HairColor = "Blue"}
};
```

The following expressions all evaluate to true:

```
People.Name == {"Mary", "John", "Fritz"}
People.HairColor == {"Brown", "Brown", "Blue"}
People.HairColor.Distinct == {"Brown", "Blue"}
```

Note that the returned collection may have duplicates. To obtain a duplicate free collection, use `Distinct`.

The expression:

```
Collection.MemberField
```

is equivalent to:

```
from c in Collection
select c.MemberField
```

In the event that the identifier for the projector is equal to a member on collection, the projector is not added. Specifically, `Choose`, `Count`, and `Distinct` will not be added as projectors.

3.7.5 Uniqueness

Collections in M may contain multiple copies of the same element. The constraint `unique value` limits the number of elements in a collection with that field or fields of the same value to 1. No two elements in the collection will return true for `==`.

The unique constraint may also take an expression or a comma separated list of expressions. In this case, the constraint will ensure no two elements are equal on every expression in the list.

3.8 Null

`Null` is a type with a single value `null`. It is used in conjunction with other types to add `null` to the value space and make a nullable type. Nullable types can be specified with the postfix operator `?` or with a union of the type and `Null`.

The following type has two nullable fields, `SSN` and `Spouse`:

```
type Person {
    Name : Text;
    SSN : Text?;
    Spouse : Person | Null;
}
```

Nullability is idempotent. `T??` is the same as `T?` Collections cannot be made nullable; therefore, `T*?` is not a legal type. Elements of collections can be nullable, so `T?*` is a legal type.

Except as noted binary operations defined to take a left operand of `T`, right operand of `S` and return type of R are lifted to accept `T?`, `S?`, and return `R?`. If either actual operand is `null`, the operation will return `null`. Logical operations `&&` and `||` are not lifted.

The following binary operations take `Null` as a left operand.

Operator	Right Operand	Return
== !=	Null	Logical
??	Any	Any

The return type of `??` is specialized to the type for the left operand without the `null` value. The type of the right operand must be compatible with the type of the left operand.

The default value of type `Null` is `null`.

CHAPTER 4

COMPUTED AND STORED VALUES

M provides two primary means for values to come into existence: computed values and stored values (aka fields). Computed and stored values may occur with both module and entity declarations and are scoped by their container.

A computed value is derived from evaluating an expression. In contrast, a field stores a value and the contents of the field may change over time.[1]

4.1 Computed Value Declaration

A *ComputedValueDeclaration* binds a name to an expression that is used to compute the resultant value.

ComputedValueDeclaration:

   Identifier FormalParameters ReturnType$_{opt}$ ExpressionBody

FormalParameters:

   (*Parameters$_{opt}$*)

Parameters:

   Parameter

   Parameters , Parameter

Parameter:

   Identifier TypeAscription$_{opt}$

ReturnType:

   TypeAscription

ExpressionBody:

   { *Expression ;$_{opt}$* }

---

[1] M currently provides no language constructs for mutating the contents of a field. However, implementations are likely to provide out-of-band mechanisms for update.

If the type of a parameter or the *ReturnType* is not explicitly specified, the parameter or return type will be implicitly inferred from the *ExpressionBody*. For example, the following *ComputedValueDeclaration*s have the same meaning:

```
Add(x : Integer32, y : Integer32) { x + y }
Add(x : Integer32, y : Integer32) : Integer32 { x + y }
```

ComputedValueDeclaration introduces the formal parameters into scope. It is an error to have more than one formal parameter with the same *Identifier*.

4.1.1 Overloading

An entity may define multiple computed values with the same name. In this case, selection is determined based on arity. It is an error to define two computed values with the same name and the same arity.

At the module level, the names of computed values and fields must be disjointed.

4.2 Fields

A field is a storage location. A field declaration specifies the name of the field and optionally a type ascription that constrains values in the field to be of the ascribed type. An initial value may be defined by either equating the field with an `Expression` or using an *InitializationExpression* (Section 5.3).

If an initializer is present without a *TypeAscription*, the type of the field is the type of the initializer. If both an initializer and *TypeAscription* are present, then the initializer must conform to the *TypeAscription*.

FieldDeclaration:

   DottedIdentifer TypeAscriptionopt = *Expression* ;

   DottedIdentifer TypeAscriptionopt InitializationExpression ;*opt*

   DottedIdentifer TypeAscriptionopt ;

DottedIdentifer

   IdentifierPath

   . *IdentifierPath*

IdentifierPath

   Identifier

   IdentifierPath . *Identifier*

CHAPTER 5

EXPRESSIONS

An expression is a sequence of operators and operands. This chapter defines the syntax, order of evaluation of operands and operators, and meaning of expressions.

5.1 Operators

Expressions are constructed from operands and operators. The operators of an expression indicate which operations to apply to the operands. Examples of operators include +, -, *, and /. Examples of operands include literals, fields, and expressions.

There are the following kinds of operators:

- Unary operators take one operand and use prefix notation such as -x.
- Binary operators take two operands and use infix notation such as x + y.
- Ternary operator. Only one ternary operator, ?:, exists; it takes three operands and uses infix notation (c? x: y).
- Query comprehensions.

The order of evaluation of operators in an expression is constrained by the precedence and associativity of the operators. Unless otherwise specified, the order of evaluation of operands is undefined.

A single syntactic operator may have different meanings depending on the type of its operands. That is, an operator may be overloaded. In this case, the meaning and the return type is determined by selecting the most specific super type for both operands for which a meaning and return type are specified in Chapter 3.

5.1.1 Operator Precedence and Associativity

Precedence and associativity determine how operators and operands are grouped together. For example, the expression x + y * z is evaluated as x + (y * z) because the * operator has higher precedence than +. The following table summarizes all operators in order of precedence from highest to lowest.

Category	Operators
Primary	`x.y  f(x)`
Unary	`+  -  !  ~  # identity unique`
Multiplicity (unary postfix)	`?  +  *  #`
Multiplicative	`*  /  %`
Additive	`+  -`
Shift	`<<  >>`
Relational and type testing	`<  >  <=  >=  in x:T`
Equality	`==  !=`
Logical And (conjunction)	`&&`
Logical Or (disjunction)	`||`
Null Coalescing	`??`
Conditional	`?:`
Query Comprehension	`from  join  let  where  select  group by  accumulate`
Where	`where`
Select	`select`
Bitwise And, Intersection	`&`
Bitwise Exclusive Or	`^`
Bitwise Or, Union	`|`

When an operand occurs between two operators with the same precedence, the associativity of the operators controls the order in which the operations are performed. All binary operators are left associative, that is, operations are performed left to right. For example, `x + y + z` is evaluated as `(x + y) + z`.

Precedence and associativity can be controlled using parentheses. For example, `x + y * z` first multiplies `y` by `z` and then adds the result to `x`, but `(x + y) * z` first adds `x` and `y` and then multiplies the result by `z`.

5.2 Member Access

A *MemberAccessExpression* takes an expression that resolves to a scope as the left operand and a symbol as the right operand. Evaluating the expression returns the value bound to the symbol in the scope.

MemberAccessExpression:

   PrimaryExpression **.** *MemberName*

MemberName:

   Identifier

A *MemberAccessExpression* consists of a *PrimaryExpression*, followed by a "*.*" token, followed by a member selector. Consider the following *MemberAccessExpression*:

```
{Name = "Bill", Age = 23}.Age
```

The member access operator looks up the symbol `Age` in the scope defined by the instance:

```
{Name = "Bill", Age = 23}
```

5.2.1 Symbol Lookup

A symbol lookup is the process whereby the meaning of a name in a context is determined. A symbol lookup may occur as part of evaluating a `SimpleName` or a `MemberAccess` in an expression.

   M is a lexically scoped language. Scopes introduce symbols and may nest, and an inner scope may introduce a symbol that hides a symbol in an outer scope. Initially a symbol is resolved against the lexically innermost scope. If no matching symbol is found in the innermost scope, lookup proceeds in the containing scope. This process continues until the outermost scope is reached, which is always a module.

   The following are examples of scopes:

- An entity definition
- A module
- A field definition

- The left side of a where expression
- A query expression

A member lookup of a name N in a type T is processed as follows: The set of all accessible members named N declared in T and the base types of T is constructed. If no members named N exist and are accessible, then the lookup produces no match.

Field declarations override lexical scoping to prevent the type of a declaration binding to the declaration itself. The ascribed type of a field declaration must not be the declaration itself; however, the declaration may be used in a constraint. Consider the following example:

```
type A;
type B {
    A : A;
}
```

The lexically enclosing scope for the type ascription of the field declaration A is the entity declaration B. With no exception, the type ascription A would bind to the field declaration in a circular reference that is an error. The exception allows lexical lookup to skip the field declaration in this case.

A declaration may be used within a constraint on the ascribed type, as in the following example:

```
type Node {
    Label : Text;
    Parent : Node;
}
Nodes : Node* where item.Parent in Nodes;
```

The right operand of the in clause stipulates that the Parent field of a node must be within the collection being defined, Nodes.

5.3 Initializers

Entity types and collections use a common initialization syntax.

An *InitializationExpression* constructs a new instance of a collection or entity.

InitializationExpression:

    { *ElementInitializers*$_{opt}$ }

    { *ElementInitializers* , }

ElementInitializer:

    LeadingDottedIdentifier TypeAscription$_{opt}$ = *Expression*

    LeadingDottedIdentifer TypeAscription$_{opt}$ *InitializationExpression*

ElementInitializers:

    ElementInitializer

    ElementInitializers , *ElementInitializer*

LeadingDottedIdentifier:

    DottedIdentifier

    . *DottedIdentifier*

5.3.1 Collection Initializer

The following example initializes the extent `SmallNumbers` to the collection of values 1, 2, 3, 4:

```
SmallNumbers { 1, 2, 3, 4 }
```

5.3.2 Enumeration Initializer

The following example initializes three extents: `Colors`, `Makes`, and `Cars`. Although there is no intrinsic enumeration type in the M language, the first two extents are used as enumerations.

```
Colors { Red = "Red", Blue = "Blue", Yellow = "Yellow" }
Makes { Ford = "Ford", Chevy = "Chevrolet" }
Cars {
    { Make = Makes.Ford, Color = Colors.Blue }
    { Make = Makes.Chevy, Color = Colors.Red }
}
```

5.3.3 Reference Initializer

M provides labeled collections to construct instances that reference each other. Consider the following type `Person` and extent `People`:

```
type Person {
    Id : Integer32 = AutoNumber();
    Name : Text;
    Age : Integer32;
    Spouse : Person;
} where identity Id;


People : Person* where item.Spouse in People;
```

The `Spouse` field references another `Person`. One way to initialize this structure is to explicitly assign the identity of each instance:

```
People {
    { Id = 0, Name = "Jack", Age = 23, Spouse = 1 },
    { Id = 1, Name = "Jill", Age = 25, Spouse = 0 },
}
```

This assumes that the values 0 and 1 are not already used in the `Person` extent and exposes unnecessary implementation details. M provides label values to initialize references without explicit manipulation of identity values. Consider the following example, which initializes the same preceding structure:

```
People {
    Jack { Name = "Jack", Age = 23, Spouse = Jill },
    Jill { Name = "Jill", Age = 25, Spouse = Jack },
}
```

The label `Jack` introduces an identifier that can be used to reference the instance. This allows the first instance, `Jack`, to reference the second instance, `Jill`, as a spouse and *vice versa*.

5.3.4 Non-Local Initialization

It is frequently useful to initialize a value in another structure. In the following example, computers have zero to many boards. This relationship is implemented as a reference from `Board` to `Computer`.

```
type Computer {
    Id : Integer32 = AutoNumber();
    Processor : Text;
} where identity Id;

type Board {
    Id : Integer32 = AutoNumber();
    Kind : Text;
    Computer : Computer;
} where identity Id;

Boards : Board* where item.Computer in Computers;
Computers : Computer*;
```

Creating an instance of a computer requires initializing both the computer and the boards. This can be initialized "bottom up" as follows:

```
Computers {
    MyPC { Processor = "x86"}
}


Boards {
    { Kind = "Graphics", Computer = Computers.MyPC },
    { Kind = "Sound", Computer = Computers.MyPC },
    { Kind = "Network", Computer = Computers.MyPC },
}
```

Using non-local initialization, this same structure can be initialized "top down" as follows:

```
Computers {
    MyPC { Processor = "x86",
            .Boards {
                { Kind = "Graphics", Computer = MyPC },
                { Kind = "Sound", Computer = MyPC },
                { Kind = "Network", Computer = MyPC },
            }
    }
}
```

The dot prefix to the Boards label (`.Boards`) does not introduce a new label into the current scope. Rather, it looks up the symbol at the extent scope and adds the content to that extent.

5.4 Invocation Expression

The Identifier in an *InvocationExpression* resolves to a computed value declaration of the same name and arity. Evaluating an invocation expression causes each argument to be evaluated. The result of each argument is bound to the formal parameter in the corresponding position. The result of evaluating the body of the computed value declaration is the value of the invocation expression:

InvocationExpression:

    Identifier InvocationExpressionArguments

InvocationExpressionArguments:

    (*Arguments$_{opt}$*)

Arguments:

    Argument

    Arguments , Argument

Argument:

    Expression

5.5 Primary Expressions

The following rules define the grammar for primary expressions:

PrimaryExpression:

    PrimaryCreationExpression

PrimaryCreationExpression:

    Literal

    SimpleName

ParenthesizedExpression

MemberAccessExpression

InvocationExpression

InitializationExpression

EntityTypeExpression

ContextVariable

Literal is defined in Section 2.4.3. *EntityTypeExpression* is defined in Section 3.6. The remaining non-terminals are defined in this section.

5.5.1 Simple Names

A *SimpleName* consists of a single identifier.

SimpleName:

   Identifier

In the expression:

```
Person.Age
```

Both `Person` and `Age` are *SimpleNames*.

5.5.2 Parenthesized Expressions

A *ParenthesizedExpression* consists of an *Expression* enclosed in parentheses:

ParenthesizedExpression:

  (*Expression*)

A *ParenthesizedExpression* is evaluated by evaluating the *Expression* within the parentheses.

5.6 Context Variable

The following rules define the grammar for context variables:

ContextVariable

```
this

value

item
```

The context variable `this` is defined in Section 3.2. `value` and `item` are defined in Section 5.16.1.

5.7 Unary Operators

The following rules define the grammar for unary operators:

UnaryExpression:

>*PrimaryExpression*
>
>+ *PrimaryExpression*
>
>− *PrimaryExpression*
>
>! *PrimaryExpression*
>
>~ *PrimaryExpression*
>
>*PrimaryExpression* #
>
>*IdentityExpression*
>
>*UniqueExpression*

IdentityExpression:

```
identity Identifier

identity ( Identifiers )
```

UniqueExpression:

```
unique Identifier

unique ( Identifiers )
```

The identity constraint is discussed in Section 3.6.2.

The type rules for unary operators are defined in Number (Section 3.5.3.1), Logical (Section 3.5.6), Binary (Section 3.5.7), and Collection (Section 3.7.2).

Examples of unary operators follow:

```
+1
-2
!true
~0x00
{1,2,3}#
identity Id
unique Name
```

5.8 Multiplicity

The following rules define the grammar for multiplicity operators:

MultiplicityExpression:

   UnaryExpression

   UnaryExpression ?

   UnaryExpression +

   UnaryExpression *

   UnaryExpression # *IntegralRange*

IntegralRange:

   IntegerLiteral

   IntegerLiteral ..

   IntegerLiteral .. *IntegerLiteral*

The type rules for multiplicity operators are defined in type operators in Section 3.4.

Examples of multiplicity expressions follow:

```
Integer32?
Text#2..4
{Name : Text; Age : Integer32}*
```

5.9 Arithmetic Operators

The following rules define the grammar for arithmetic operators:

AdditiveExpression:

   MultiplicativeExpression

   AdditiveExpression + MultiplicativeExpression

   AdditiveExpression – MultiplicativeExpression

MultiplicativeExpression:

   UnaryExpression

   *MultiplicativeExpression * MultiplicityExpression*

   MultiplicativeExpression / MultiplicityExpression

   MultiplicativeExpression % MultiplicityExpression

The type rules on arithmetic operators are defined in Number (Section 3.5.3), Text (Section 3.5.4), Date (Section 3.5.9), and Time (Section 3.5.11).
    Examples of arithmetic operators follow:

```
1 + 1
2 * 3
"Hello " + "World"
```

5.10 Shift Operators

The following rules define the grammar for shift operators:

ShiftExpression:

   AdditiveExpression

   ShiftExpression << AdditiveExpression

   ShiftExpression >> AdditiveExpression

The type rules on shift operators are defined in Binary, Section 3.5.7.

5.11 Relational and Type-Testing Operators

The following rules define the grammar for relational and type testing operators:

RelationalExpression:

  ShiftExpression

  RelationalExpression < *ShiftExpression*

  RelationalExpression > *ShiftExpression*

  RelationalExpression <= *ShiftExpression*

  RelationalExpression >= *ShiftExpression*

  RelationalExpression in *ShiftExpression*

  RelationalExpression : *ShiftExpression*

The type rules on relational and type-testing operators are throughout Chapter 3.

5.12 Equality Operators

The following rules define the grammar for equality operators:

EqualityExpression:

  RelationalExpression

  EqualityExpression == *RelationalExpression*

  EqualityExpression != *RelationalExpression*

The type rules on equality operators are throughout Chapter 3.

5.13 Logical Operators

The following rules define the grammar for logical operators.

LogicalAndExpression:

  EqualityExpression

  LogicalAndExpression && *EqualityExpression*

LogicalOrExpression:

   LogicalAndExpression

   LogicalOrExpression || *LogicalAndExpression*

The type rules on logical operators are defined in Logical, Section 3.5.6.

5.14 Conditional Operators

There are two conditional operators: coalesce and conditional.

5.14.1 Coalescing Operator

The ?? operator is called the null coalescing operator:

NullCoalescingExpression:

   LogicalOrExpression

   LogicalOrExpression ?? *NullCoalescingExpression*

A null coalescing expression of the form a ?? b requires a to be nullable. If a is not null, the result of a ?? b is a; otherwise, the result is b. The operation evaluates b only if a is null.

   b must be of the same type as a without the value null.

5.14.2 Conditional Operator

The ?: operator is called the conditional operator. It is at times also called the ternary operator.

ConditionalExpression:

   NullCoalescingExpression

   NullCoalescingExpression ? *Expression* : *Expression*

A conditional expression of the form b ? x : y first evaluates the condition b. Then, if b is true, x is evaluated and becomes the result of the operation. Otherwise, y is evaluated and becomes the result of the operation. A conditional expression never evaluates both x and y.

The conditional operator is right-associative, meaning that operations are grouped from right to left. For example, an expression of form `a ? b : c ? d : e` is evaluated as `a ? b : (c ? d : e)`.

The first operand of the `?:` operator must be an expression of a type that can be implicitly converted to `Logical`; otherwise a compile-time error occurs. The middle and left operands must be of compatible types. The result of the conditional is the least specific type.

5.15 Query Expressions

Query expressions provide a language integrated syntax for queries that is similar to relational and hierarchical query languages such as Transact SQL and XQuery.

A query expression begins with a `from` clause and ends with either a `select`, `group`, or `accumulate` clause. The initial `from` clause can be followed by zero or more `from`, `let`, or `where` clauses. Each `from` clause is a scope that introduces one or more iteration identifiers ranging over a sequence or a join of multiple sequences. Each `let` clause computes a value and introduces an identifier representing that value, and each `where` clause is a filter that excludes items from the result that do not satisfy the `Logical` expression. The final `select`, `accumulate`, or `group` clause specifies the shape of the result in terms of the iteration identifiers(s). Finally, an `into` clause can be used to "splice" queries by treating the results of one query as a generator in a subsequent query:

QueryExpression:

    ConditionalExpression

    QueryFromClause QueryBody

QueryBody:

    QueryBodyClauses$_{opt}$ QueryConstructor QueryContinuation$_{opt}$

QueryBodyClauses:

    QueryBodyClause

    QueryBodyClauses QueryBodyClause

QueryBodyClause:

    QueryFromClause

    QueryLetClause

QueryWhereClause

QueryJoinClause

QueryJoinIntoClause

QueryConstructor:

QuerySelectClause

QueryGroupClause

QueryAccumulateClause

QueryContinuation:

into *Identifier QueryBody*

QueryFromClause:

from *Identifier* in *ConditionalExpression*

QueryLetClause:

let *Identifier* = *ConditionalExpression*

QueryJoinClause:

join *Identifier* in *Expression* on *Expression* equals *ConditionalExpression*

QueryJoinIntoClause:

join *Identifier* in *Expression* on *Expression* equals *Expression* into *Identifier*

QueryWhereClause:

where *ConditionalExpression*

QuerySelectClause:

select *ConditionalExpression*

QueryGroupClause:

group *Expression* by *ConditionalExpression*

QueryAccumulateClause:

QueryLetClause accumulate *ConditionalExpression*

The accumulate keyword generalizes Sum, Min, Max, et cetera. Its purpose is to repeatedly apply an expression to each element in a collection and accumulate the result. Consider the following fragment:

```
from c in CollectionExpression
let a = Expression
accumulate Expression
```

As an example, the following M code sums the elements in the collection Numbers:

```
from n in Numbers
let i = 0
accumulate i + n
```

5.16 Compact Query Expressions

There are two compact forms for query expressions the binary infix `where` and `select`.

5.16.1 Where Operator

The infix `where` operation filters elements from a collection that match a predicate:

WhereExpression:

   QueryExpression

   QueryExpression `where` *WhereExpressions*

WhereExpressions:

   WhereExpression

   WhereExpressions `,` *WhereExpression*

The *WhereExpression* introduces the identifier `value` into the scope of the right side to refer to an element of the collection on the left. The right side may also use any other identifiers that are in lexical scope.

If the *QueryExpression* returns a collection of collections (e.g. `Number*`); then the right side also introduces the identifier `item` into scope to refer to elements of the base domain.

The following example uses `value` to filter the Numbers collection:

```
OneToTen : Number where value > 0 && value <= 10;
```

When used over a collection type, value refers to the collection:

```
SmallCollection : Number* where value.Count == 2;

SmallCollectionOneToTen : (Number where value > 0 && value <=10)*
    where value.Count < 10;
```

The keyword item constrains the values of elements of elements. The following declaration is equivalent to the previous:

```
SmallCollectionOneToTen : Number* where value.Count < 10 &&
    item > 0 &&
    item <= 10;
```

Formalizing this convention:

QueryExpression `where` *Expression*

is a compact syntax for one of the two following expressions:

```
from value in QueryExpression
where Expression
select value
```

```
from value in QueryExpression
where (from item in value select Expression).All
select value
```

The choice between the first and second expansions is made based on the type of the left operand to the `where` clause. If it is a collection of collections the second expansion is used; otherwise, if it is a collection, the first expansion is used; otherwise it is a type error.

5.16.2 Select Operator

The select operator applies an expression to every element in a collection and returns the results in a new collection:

SelectExpression:

   WhereExpression

   WhereExpression `select` *Expression*

The *SelectExpression* introduces the identifier value into the scope of the right side to refer to an element of the collection on the left. The right side may also use any other identifiers that are in lexical scope.

   Examples of the select operator follow:

```
{1, 2, 3} select value * 2
People select value.Name
{{}, {1}, {1,1}} select value#
```

5.17 Binary and Collection Operators

The following rules define the grammar for binary and collection operators:

InclusiveOrExpression:

  ExclusiveOrExpression

  InclusiveOrExpression | ExclusiveOrExpression

ExclusiveOrExpression:

  AndExpression

  ExclusiveOrExpression ^ AndExpression

AndExpression:

  SelectExpression

  AndExpression & SelectExpression

The type rules on binary and collection operators are defined in Binary, Section 3.5.7, and Collection, Section 3.7.2.

5.18 Expressions

An expression is a sequence of operands and operators. Applying the operator to the operand yields a value:

Expression:

InclusiveOrExpression

CHAPTER 6

MODULE

A module is a scope that contains declarations of types (Chapter 3), extents (Section 4.2), and computed values (Section 4.1). Modules override lexical scoping to import symbols that have been exported from another module.

6.1 Compilation Unit

Several modules may be contained within a *CompilationUnit*, typically a text file.

CompilationUnit:

   ModuleDeclarationList

ModuleDeclarationList:

   ModuleDeclaration

   ModuleDeclarationList ModuleDeclaration

6.2 Module Declaration

A *ModuleDeclaration* is a named container/scope for type declarations, field declarations, and computed value declarations.

ModuleDeclaration:

   module *QualifiedIdentifer ModuleBody* ; $_{opt}$

QualifiedIdentifier:

   Identifier

   QualifiedIdentifier . *Identifier*

ModuleBody:

  { *ImportDirective* ExportDirective* ModuleMemberDeclaration** }

ModuleMemberDeclaration:

  FieldDeclaration

  ComputedValueDeclaration

  TypeDeclaration

Each *ModuleDeclaration* has a *QualifiedIdentifier* that uniquely qualifies the declarations contained by the module.

    Each *ModuleMemberDeclaration* may be referenced either by its *Identifier* or by its fully qualified name by concatenating the *QualifiedIdentifier* of the *ModuleDeclaration* with the *Identifier* of the *ModuleMemberDeclaration* (separated by a period).

    For example, given the following *ModuleDeclaration*:

```
module PeopleData {
    Names : Text*;
}
```

the fully qualified name of the field is `PeopleData.Names`, or using escaped identifiers, `[PeopleData].[Names]`. It is always legal to use a fully qualified name where the name of a declaration is expected.

    Modules are not hierarchical or nested. That is, there is no implied relationship between modules whose *QualifiedIdentifier* share a common prefix.

    For example, consider these two declarations:

```
module A {
    N : Number;
}
module A.B {
    NPlusOne : { N + 1 }
}
```

Module `A.B` is in error, as it does not contain a declaration for the identifier `N`. That is, the members of Module `A` are not implicitly imported into Module `A.B`.

6.3 Inter-Module Dependencies

M uses *ImportDirectives* and *ExportDirectives* to explicitly control which declarations may be used across module boundaries.

ExportDirective:

   export *Identifiers* ;

ImportDirective:

   import *ImportModules* ;

   import *QualifiedIdentifier* { *ImportMembers* } ;

ImportMember:

   Identifier ImportAlias$_{opt}$

ImportMembers:

   ImportMember

   ImportMembers , *ImportMember*

ImportModule:

   QualifiedIdentifier ImportAlias$_{opt}$

ImportModules:

   ImportModule

   ImportModules , *ImportModule*

ImportAlias:

   as *Identifier*

A *ModuleDeclaration* contains zero or more *ExportDirectives*, each of which makes a *ModuleMemberDeclaration* available to declarations outside of the current module.

   A *ModuleDeclaration* contains zero or more *ImportDirectives*, each of which names a *ModuleDeclaration* whose declarations may be referenced by the current module.

   A *ModuleMemberDeclaration* may only reference declarations in the current module and declarations that have an explicit *ImportDirective* in the current module.

   An *ImportDirective* is not transitive; that is, importing module *A* does not import the modules that *A* imports.

For example, consider this *ModuleDeclaration*:

```
module People.Types {
    export Person;

    SecretNumber : Number;
    type Person  { FirstName : Text; Age : Number; }
}
```

The field `People.Types.SecretNumber` may only be referenced from within the module `People.Types`. The type `People.Types.Person` may be referenced in any module that has an *ImportDirective* for module `People.Types`, as shown in this example:

```
module People.Data {
    import People.Types;
    export Names;

    Names : Text*;
    Friends : People.Types.Person*;
}
```

The preceding example used the fully qualified name to refer to `People.Types.Person`. An *ImportDirective* may also specify an *ImportAlias* that provides a replacement *Identifier* for the imported declaration:

```
module People.Data {
    import People.Types as pt;
    export Names;

    Names : Text*;
    Friends : pt.Person*;
}
```

An *ImportAlias* replaces the name of the imported declaration. That means that the following is an error:

```
module People.Data {
    import People.Types as pt;
    export Names;
```

```
    Names : Text*;
    Friends : People.Types.Person*;
}
```

It is legal for two or more *ImportDirectives* to import the same declaration, provided they specify distinct aliases. For a given compilation episode, at most one *ImportDirective* may use a given alias.

If an *ImportDirective* imports a module without specifying an alias, the declarations in the imported module may be referenced without the qualification of the module name. That means the following is also legal:

```
module People.Data {
    import People.Types;
    export Names;

    Names : Text*;
    Friends : Person*;
}
```

When two modules contain same-named declarations, there is a potential for ambiguity. The potential for ambiguity is not an error—ambiguity errors are detected lazily as part of resolving references.

Consider the following two modules:

```
module A {
    export X;
    X : Number;
}
module B {
    export X;
    X : Number;
}
```

It is legal to import both modules either with or without providing an alias:

```
module C {
    import A, B;
    Y { 1 + 2 }
}
```

This is legal because ambiguity is only an error for references, not declarations. That means that the following is a compile-time error:

```
module C {
    import A, B;
    Y { X + 2 } // error: unqualified identifier X is ambiguous
}
```

This example can be made legal either by fully qualifying the reference to X:

```
module C {
    import A, B;
    Y { A.X + 2 } // no error
}
```

or by adding an alias to one or both of the *ImportDirectives*:

```
module C {
    import A;
    import B as bb;
    Y { X + 2 } // no error, refers to A.X
    Z { bb.X + 2 } // no error, refers to B.X
}
```

Because module names may contain periods, there is a potential ambiguity when module names share a common prefix. Consider these two modules:

```
module A {
    export Z, B;
    type Z { C : Number; }
    B : Z;
}
module A.B {
    export C;
    C : Number;
}
```

If a module imports both of these modules, the *QualifiedIdentifier* A.B.C is inherently ambiguous, as it could either refer to the C field in module A.B or to the C field of the B field of module A. To disambiguate, one must use an alias to break the tie:

```
module F {
    import A;
    import A.B as ab;
    G { ab.C } // returns the C field of module A.B
    H { A.B.C }  // returns the C field of the B field of module A
}
```

An *ImportDirective* may either import all exported declarations from a module or only one of them. The latter is enabled by specifying an *ImportMember* as part of the directive. For example, Module Plot2D imports only Point2D and PointPolar from the Module Geometry:

```
module Geometry {
    export Point2D, Point2DPolar, Point3D;
    type Point2D { X : Number; Y : Number; }
    type Point2DPolar { R : Number; T : Number; }
    type Point3D : Point2D { Z : Number; }
}
module Plot2D {
    import Geometry {Point2D, Point2DPolar};
    Points : Point2D*;
    PointsPolar : Point2DPolar*;
}
```

An *ImportDirective* that contains an *ImportMember* only imports the named declarations from that module. This means that the following is a compilation error because module Plot3D references Point3D, which is not imported from module Geometry:

```
module Plot3D {
    import Geometry {Point2D};
    Points : Point3D*;
}
```

An *ImportDirective* that contains an *ImportTarget* and an *ImportAlias* assign the replacement name to the imported type, field, or computed value declaration.

6.4 Compilation Episode

Multiple compilation units may contribute declarations to a module of the same name.

The types and computed values of a module are sealed by a compilation episode. A subsequent compilation episode may not contribute additional types or computed values. Initial values for module level field declarations may be contributed in subsequent compilation episodes.

Each fragment must explicitly import the symbols used within that fragment and may only export symbols defined within that fragment.

6.5 Storage

All dynamic storage in M is modeled as module-scoped *FieldDeclarations* called extents. The declaration of an extent may be spread across multiple sections of program text. Consider the following example:

```
// catalog.m
module Catalog {
    type Product {
        Name : Text;
        Price : Decimal9;
        Product(Name,Price);
    }

    Products : Product*;
}

// groceries.m
module Catalog {
    Products {
        Product("Soap", 1.29),
        Product("Tuna", 2.49)
    }
```

```
}

// hardware.m
module Catalog {
    Products {
        Product("Lightbulb", 0.99),
        Product("Screwdriver", 5.99)
    }
}
```

The resulting Products extent will contain:

```
{
    Product("Soap", 1.29),
    Product("Tuna", 2.49),
    Product("Lightbulb", 0.99),
    Product("Screwdriver", 5.99)
}
```

The mapping of module-scoped *FieldDeclarations* to physical storage is implementation-specific and outside the scope of this specification.

MGrammar Language Specification

CHAPTER 7

INTRODUCTION TO MGRAMMAR LANGUAGE

Text is often the most natural way to represent information for presentation and editing by people. However, the ability to extract that information for use by software has been an arcane art practiced only by the most advanced developers. The success of XML is evidence that there is significant demand for using text to represent information—this evidence is even more compelling considering the relatively poor readability of XML syntax and the decade-long challenge to make XML-based information easily accessible to programs and stores. The emergence of simpler technologies like JSON and the growing use of meta-programming facilities in Ruby to build textual domain specific languages (DSLs) such as Ruby on Rails or Rake speak to the desire for natural textual representations of information. However, even these technologies limit the expressiveness of the representation by relying on fixed formats to encode all information uniformly, resulting in text that has very few visual cues from the problem domain (much like XML).

The MGrammar Language (M_g) was created to enable information to be represented in a textual form that is tuned for both the problem domain and the target audience. The M_g language provides simple constructs for describing the shape of a textual language—that shape includes the input syntax as well as the structure and contents of the underlying information. To that end, M_g acts as both a schema language that can validate that textual input conforms to a given language as well as a transformation language that projects textual input into data structures that are amenable to further processing or storage. The data that results from M_g processing is compatible with M_g's sister language, the "Oslo" Modeling Language, "M," which provides a SQL-compatible schema and query language that can be used to further process the underlying information.

7.1 Language Basics

An M_g-based language definition consists of one or more named rules, each of which describe some part of the language. The following fragment is a simple language definition:

```
language HelloLanguage {
  syntax Main = "Hello, World";
}
```

The language being specified is named `HelloLanguage` and it is described by one rule named `Main`. A language may contain more than one rule; the name `Main` is used to designate the initial rule that all input documents must match in order to be considered valid with respect to the language.

Rules use patterns to describe the set of input values that the rule applies to. The `Main` rule above has only one pattern, `"Hello, World"`, that describes exactly one legal input value:

```
Hello, World
```

If that input is fed to the M_g processor for this language, the processor will report that the input is valid. Any other input will cause the processor to report the input as invalid.

Typically, a rule will use multiple patterns to describe alternative input formats that are logically related. For example, consider this language:

```
language PrimaryColors {
  syntax Main = "Red" | "Green" | "Blue";
}
```

The `Main` rule has three patterns—input must conform to one of these patterns in order for the rule to apply. That means that the following is valid:

```
Red
```

as well as this:

```
Green
```

and this:

```
Blue
```

No other input values are valid in this language.

Most patterns in the wild are more expressive than those we've seen so far—most patterns combine multiple terms. Every pattern consists of a sequence of one or more grammar terms, each of which describes a set of legal text values. Pattern matching has the effect of consuming the input as it sequentially matches the terms in the pattern. Each term in the pattern consumes zero or more initial characters of input—the remainder of the input is then matched against the next term in the pattern. If all of the terms in a pattern cannot be matched, the consumption is "undone" and the original input will used as a candidate for matching against other patterns within the rule.

A pattern term can either specify a literal value (like in our first example) or the name of another rule. The following language definition matches the same input as the first example:

```
language HelloLanguage2 {
  syntax Main = Prefix ", " Suffix;
  syntax Prefix = "Hello";
  syntax Suffix = "World";
}
```

Like functions in a traditional programming language, rules can be declared to accept parameters. A parameterized rule declares one or more "holes" that must be specified to use the rule. The following is a parameterized rule:

```
syntax Greeting(salutation, separator) = salutation separator "World";
```

To use a parameterized rule, one simply provides actual rules as arguments to be substituted for the declared parameters:

```
syntax Main = Greeting(Prefix, ", ");
```

A given rule name may be declared multiple times provided each declaration has a different number of parameters. That is, the following is legal:

```
syntax Greeting(salutation, sep, subject) = salutation sep subject;
syntax Greeting(salutation, sep) = salutation sep "World";
```

```
syntax Greeting(sep) = "Hello" sep "World";
syntax Greeting = "Hello" ", " "World";
```

The selection of which rule is used is determined based on the number of arguments present in the usage of the rule.

A pattern may indicate that a given term may match repeatedly using the standard Kleene operators (e.g. ?, *, and +). For example, consider this language:

```
language HelloLanguage3 {
   syntax Main = Prefix ", "? Suffix*;
   syntax Prefix = "Hello";
   syntax Suffix = "World";
}
```

This language considers all the following to be valid:

```
Hello
Hello,
Hello, World
Hello, WorldWorld
HelloWorldWorldWorld
```

Terms can be grouped using parentheses to indicate that a group of terms must be repeated:

```
language HelloLanguage3 {
   syntax Main = Prefix (", " Suffix)+;
   syntax Prefix = "Hello";
   syntax Suffix = "World";
}
```

which considers all the following to be valid input:

```
Hello, World
Hello, World, World
Hello, World, World, World
```

The use of the + operator indicates that the group of terms must match at least once.

7.2 Character Processing

In the previous examples of the `HelloLanguage`, the pattern term for the comma separator included a trailing space. That trailing space was significant, as it allowed the input text to include a space after the comma:

```
Hello, World
```

More importantly, the pattern indicates that the space is not only allowed, but is required. That is, the following input is not valid:

```
Hello,World
```

Moreover, exactly one space is required, making this input invalid as well:

```
Hello,    World
```

To allow any number of spaces to appear either before or after the comma, we could have written the rule like this:

```
syntax Main = 'Hello'  ' '*    ','  ' '*  'World';
```

While this is correct, in practice most languages have many places where secondary text, such as whitespace or comments, can be interleaved with constructs that are primary in the language. To simplify specifying such languages, a language may specify one or more named interleave patterns.

   An interleave pattern specifies text streams that are not considered part of the primary flow of text. When processing input, the M_g processor implicitly injects interleave patterns between the terms in all syntax patterns. For example, consider this language:

```
language HelloLanguage {
  syntax Main = "Hello"   ","    "World";
  interleave Secondary = " "+;
}
```

This language now accepts any number of whitespace characters before or after the comma. That is,

```
Hello,World
Hello, World
Hello    ,                 World
```

are all valid with respect to this language.

Interleave patterns simplify defining languages that have secondary text like whitespace and comments. However, many languages have constructs in which such interleaving needs to be suppressed. To specify that a given rule is not subject to interleave processing, the rule is written as a token rule rather than a syntax rule.

Token rules identify the lowest level textual constructs in a language—by analogy token rules identify words, and syntax rules identify sentences. Like syntax rules, token rules use patterns to identify sets of input values. Here's a simple token rule:

```
token BinaryValueToken  = ("0" | "1")+;
```

It identifies sequences of 0 and 1 characters much like this similar syntax rule:

```
syntax BinaryValueSyntax = ("0" | "1")+;
```

The main distinction between the two rules is that interleave patterns do not apply to token rules. That means that if the following interleave rule was in effect:

```
interleave IgnorableText = " "+;
```

then the following input value:

```
0 1011 1011
```

would be valid with respect to the BinaryValueSyntax rule but not with respect to the BinaryValueToken rule, as interleave patterns do not apply to token rules.

M_g provides a shorthand notation for expressing alternatives that consist of a range of Unicode characters. For example, the following rule:

```
token AtoF = "A" | "B" | "C" | "D" | "E" | "F";
```

can be rewritten using the range operator as follows:

```
token AtoF = "A".."F";
```

Ranges and alternation can compose to specify multiple non-contiguous ranges:

```
token AtoGnoD = "A".."C" | "E".."G";
```

which is equivalent to this longhand form:

```
token AtoGnoD = "A" | "B" | "C" | "E" | "F" | "G";
```

Note that the range operator only works with text literals that are exactly one character in length.

The patterns in token rules have a few additional features that are not valid in syntax rules. Specifically, token patterns can be negated to match anything not included in the set, by using the difference operator (-). The following example combines difference with any. Any matches any single character. The expression below matches any character that is not a vowel:

```
any - ('A'|'E'|'I'|'O'|'U')
```

Token rules are named and may be referred to by other rules:

```
token AorBorCorEorForG = (AorBorC | EorForG)+;
token AorBorC = 'A'..'C';
token EorForG = 'E'..'G';
```

Because token rules are processed before syntax rules, token rules cannot refer to syntax rules:

```
syntax X = "Hello";
token HelloGoodbye = X | "Goodbye"; // illegal
```

However, syntax rules may refer to token rules:

```
token X = "Hello";
syntax HelloGoodbye = X | "Goodbye"; // legal
```

The M_g processor treats all literals in syntax patterns as anonymous token rules. That means that the previous example is equivalent to the following:

```
token X = "Hello";
token temp = "Goodbye";
syntax HelloGoodbye = X | temp;
```

Operationally, the difference between token rules and syntax rules is when they are processed. Token rules are processed first against the raw character stream to produce a sequence of named tokens. The M_g processor then processes the language's syntax rules against the token stream to determine whether the input is valid and optionally to produce structured data as output. The next section describes how that output is formed.

7.3 Output

M_g processing transforms text into structured data. The shape and content of that data is determined by the syntax rules of the language being processed. Each syntax rule consists of a set of productions, each of which consists of a pattern and an optional projection. Patterns, which were discussed in the previous sections, describe a set of legal character sequences that are valid input. Projections describe how the information represented by that input should be produced.

Each production is like a function from text to structured data. The primary way to write projections is to use a simple construction syntax that produces graph-structured data suitable for programs and stores. For example, consider this rule:

```
syntax Rock =
    "Rock" => Item { Heavy { true }, Solid { true } } ;
```

This rule has one production that has a pattern that matches `"Rock"` and a projection that produces the following value (using a notation known as D graphs):

```
Item {
  Heavy { true },
  Solid { true }
}
```

Rules can contain more than one production in order to allow different input to produce very different output. Here's an example of a rule that contains three productions with very different projections:

```
syntax Contents
    = "Rock" => Item { Heavy { true }, Solid { true } }
    | "Water" => Item { Consumable { true }, Solid { false } }
    | "Hamster" => Pet { Small { true }, Legs { 4 } } ;
```

When a rule with more than one production is processed, the input text is tested against all of the productions in the rule to determine whether the rule applies. If the input text matches the pattern from exactly one of the rule's productions, then the corresponding projection is used to produce the result. In this example, when presented with the input text `"Hamster"`, the rule would yield:

```
Pet {
  Small { true },
  Legs { 4 }
}
```

as a result.

To allow a syntax rule to match no matter what input it is presented with, a syntax rule may specify a production that uses the `empty` pattern, which will be selected if and only if none of the other productions in the rule match:

```
syntax Contents
    = "Rock" => Item { Heavy { true }, Solid { true } }
    | "Water" => Item { Consumable { true }, Solid { false } }
    | "Hamster" => Pet { Small { true }, Legs { 4 } }
    | empty => NoContent { } ;
```

When the production with the empty pattern is chosen, no input is consumed as part of the match.

To allow projections to use the input text that was used during pattern matching, pattern terms associate a variable name with individual pattern terms by prefixing the pattern with an identifier separated by a colon. These variable names are then made available to the projection. For example, consider this language:

```
language GradientLang {
  syntax Main
    = from:Color ", " to:Color => Gradient { Start { from }, End { to } } ;
  token Color
    = "Red" | "Green" | "Blue";
}
```

Given this input value:

```
Red, Blue
```

the M_g processor would produce this output:

```
Gradient {
  Start { "Red" },
  End { "Blue" }
}
```

Like all projection expressions we've looked at, literal values may appear in the output graph. The set of literal types supported by M_g and a few examples follow:

- Text literals—`"ABC"`, `'ABC'`
- Integer literals—`25`, `-34`
- Real literals—`0.0`, `-5.0E15`
- Logical literals—`true`, `false`
- Null literal—`null`

The projections we've seen so far all attach a label to each graph node in the output (e.g., Gradient, Start, and so on). The label is optional and can be omitted:

```
syntax Naked = t1:First t2:Second => { t1, t2 };
```

The label can be an arbitrary string—to allow labels to be escaped, one uses the `id` operator:

```
syntax Fancy = t1:First t2:Second => id("Label with Spaces!"){ t1, t2 };
```

The `id` operator works with either literal strings or with variables that are bound to input text:

```
syntax Fancy = name:Name t1:First t2:Second => id(name){ t1, t2 };
```

Using `id` with variables allows the labeling of the output data to be driven dynamically from input text rather than statically defined in the language. This example works when the variable name is bound to a literal value. If the variable was bound to a structured node that was returned by another rule, that node's label can be accessed using the `labelof` operator:

```
syntax Fancier p:Point => id(labelof(p)) { 1, 2, 3 };
```

The `labelof` operator returns a string that can be used both in the `id` operator as well as a node value.

The projection expressions shown so far have no notion of order. That is, this projection expression:

```
A { X { 100 }, Y { 200 } }
```

is semantically equivalent to this:

```
A { Y { 200 }, X { 100 } }
```

and implementations of M_g are not required to preserve the order specified by the projection. To indicate that order is significant and must be preserved, brackets are used rather than braces. This means that this projection expression:

```
A [ X { 100 }, Y { 200 } ]
```

is *not* semantically equivalent to this:

```
A [ Y { 200 }, X { 100 } ]
```

The use of brackets is common when the sequential nature of information is important and positional access is desired in downstream processing.

Sometimes it is useful to splice the nodes of a value together into a single collection. The `valuesof` operator will return the values of a node (labeled or unlabeled) as top-level values that are then combinable with other values as values of new node.

```
syntax ListOfA
    = a:A => [a]
    | list:ListOfA "," a:A => [ valuesof(list), a ];
```

Here, `valuesof(list)` returns all the values of the `list` node, combinable with `a` to form a new list.

Productions that do not specify a projection get the default projection.

For example, consider this simple language that does not specify productions:

```
language GradientLanguage {
  syntax Main = Gradient | Color;
```

```
    syntax Gradient = from:Color " on " to:Color;
    token Color = "Red" | "Green" | "Blue";
}
```

When presented with the input `"Blue on Green"` the language processor returns the following output:

```
Main[ Gradient [ "Red", " on ", "Green" ] ] ]
```

These default semantics allow grammars to be authored rapidly while still yielding understandable output. However, in practice explicit projection expressions provide language designers complete control over the shape and contents of the output.

7.4 Modularity

All of the examples shown so far have been "loose M$_g$" that is taken out of context. To write a legal M$_g$ document, all source text must appear in the context of a *module definition*. A module defines a top-level namespace for any languages that are defined.

Here is a simple module definition:

```
module Literals {
  // declare a language
  language Number {
    syntax Main = ('0'..'9')+;
  }
}
```

In this example, the module defines one language named `Literals.Number`.

Modules may refer to declarations in other modules by using an *import directive* to name the module containing the referenced declarations. For a declaration to be referenced by other modules, the declaration must be explicitly exported using an *export directive*.

Consider this module:

```
module MyModule {
  import HerModule; // declares HerType

  export MyLanguage1;
```

```
language MyLanguage1 {
  syntax Main = HerLanguage.Options;
}
language MyLanguage2 {
  syntax Main = "x"+;
}
}
```

Note that only MyLanguage1 is visible to other modules. This makes the following definition of HerModule legal:

```
module HerModule {
  import MyModule; // declares MyLanguage1
  export HerLanguage;

  language HerLanguage {
    syntax Options = (('a'..'z')+ ('on'|'off'))*;
  }
  language Private { }
}
```

As this example shows, modules may have circular dependencies.

CHAPTER 8

LEXICAL STRUCTURE

8.1 Programs

An M_g program consists of one or more source files, known formally as compilation units. A compilation unit file is an ordered sequence of Unicode characters. Compilation units typically have a one-to-one correspondence with files in a file system, but this correspondence is not required. For maximal portability, it is recommended that files in a file system be encoded with the UTF-8 encoding.

Conceptually speaking, a program is compiled using four steps:

1. Lexical analysis, which translates a stream of Unicode input characters into a stream of tokens. Lexical analysis evaluates and executes pre-processing directives.
2. Syntactic analysis, which translates the stream of tokens into an abstract syntax tree.
3. Semantic analysis, which resolves all symbols in the abstract syntax tree, type checks the structure, and generates a semantic graph.
4. Code generation, which generates instructions from the semantic graph for some target runtime, producing an image.

Further tools may link images and load them into a runtime.

8.2 Grammars

This specification presents the syntax of the M_g programming language using two grammars. The lexical grammar defines how Unicode characters are combined to form line terminators, white space, comments, tokens, and pre-processing directives. The syntactic grammar defines how the tokens resulting from the lexical grammar are combined to form M_g programs.

8.2.1 Grammar Notation

The lexical and syntactic grammars are presented using grammar productions. Each grammar production defines a non-terminal symbol and the possible expansions of that non-terminal symbol into sequences of non-terminal or terminal symbols. In grammar productions, *non-terminal* symbols are shown in italic type, and `terminal` symbols are shown in a fixed-width font.

The first line of a grammar production is the name of the non-terminal symbol being defined, followed by a colon. Each successive indented line contains a possible expansion of the non-terminal given as a sequence of non-terminal or terminal symbols. For example, the production:

IdentifierVerbatim:

   [*IdentifierVerbatimCharacters*]

defines an *IdentifierVerbatim* to consist of the token "[", followed by *IdentifierVerbatimCharacters*, followed by the token "]".

When there is more than one possible expansion of a non-terminal symbol, the alternatives are listed on separate lines. For example, the production:

DecimalDigits:

   DecimalDigit

   DecimalDigits DecimalDigit

defines *DecimalDigits* to either consist of a *DecimalDigit* or consist of *DecimalDigits* followed by a *DecimalDigit*. In other words, the definition is recursive and specifies that a decimal-digits list consists of one or more decimal digits.

A subscripted suffix "*opt*" is used to indicate an optional symbol. The production:

DecimalLiteral:

> *IntegerLiteral* **.** *DecimalDigit DecimalDigits*_{opt}

is shorthand for:

DecimalLiteral:

> *IntegerLiteral* **.** *DecimalDigit*
>
> *IntegerLiteral* **.** *DecimalDigit DecimalDigits*

and defines a *DecimalLiteral* to consist of an *IntegerLiteral* followed by a '.' a *DecimalDigit* and by optional *DecimalDigits*.

Alternatives are normally listed on separate lines, though in cases where there are many alternatives, the phrase "one of" may precede a list of expansions given on a single line. This is simply shorthand for listing each of the alternatives on a separate line. For example, the production:

Sign: one of

> \+ –

is shorthand for:

Sign:

> \+
>
> –

Conversely, exclusions are designated with the phrase "none of". For example, the production

TextSimple: none of

> "
>
> \\
>
> *NewLineCharacter*

permits all characters except '"', '\\', and new line characters.

8.2.2 Lexical Grammar

The lexical grammar of M_g is presented in Section 8.3. The terminal symbols of the lexical grammar are the characters of the Unicode character set, and the lexical grammar specifies how characters are combined to form tokens, white space, and comments (Section 8.3.2).

Every source file in an M_g program must conform to the *Input* production of the lexical grammar.

8.2.3 Syntactic Grammar

The syntactic grammar of M_g is presented in the chapters that follow this chapter. The terminal symbols of the syntactic grammar are the tokens defined by the lexical grammar, and the syntactic grammar specifies how tokens are combined to form M_g programs.

Every source file in an M_g program must conform to the *CompilationUnit* production of the syntactic grammar.

8.3 Lexical Analysis

The *Input* production defines the lexical structure of an M_g source file. Each source file in an M_g program must conform to this lexical grammar production.

Input:
    InputSection$_{opt}$

InputSection:
    InputSectionPart
    InputSection InputSectionPart

InputSectionPart:
    InputElements$_{opt}$ *NewLine*

InputElements:
    InputElement
    InputElements InputElement

InputElement:

Whitespace

Comment

Token

Four basic elements make up the lexical structure of an M_g source file: line terminators, white space, comments, and tokens. Of these basic elements, only tokens are significant in the syntactic grammar of an M_g program.

The lexical processing of an M_g source file consists of reducing the file into a sequence of tokens, which becomes the input to the syntactic analysis. Line terminators, white space, and comments can serve to separate tokens, but otherwise these lexical elements have no impact on the syntactic structure of an M_g program.

When several lexical grammar productions match a sequence of characters in a source file, the lexical processing always forms the longest possible lexical element. For example, the character sequence // is processed as the beginning of a single-line comment because that lexical element is longer than a single / token.

8.3.1 Line Terminators

Line terminators divide the characters of an M_g source file into lines.

NewLine:

   NewLineCharacter

   U+000D   U+000A

NewLineCharacter:

   U+000A   *// Line Feed*

   U+000D   *// Carriage Return*

   U+0085   *// Next Line*

   U+2028   *// Line Separator*

   U+2029   *// Paragraph Separator*

For compatibility with source code editing tools that add end-of-file markers, and to enable a source file to be viewed as a sequence of properly terminated lines, the following transformations are applied, in order, to every compilation unit:

- If the last character of the source file is a Control-Z character (U+001A), this character is deleted.

- A carriage-return character (U+000D) is added to the end of the source file if that source file is non-empty and if the last character of the source file is not a carriage return (U+000D), a line feed (U+000A), a line separator (U+2028), or a paragraph separator (U+2029).

8.3.2 Comments

Two forms of comments are supported: single-line comments and delimited comments. Single-line comments start with the characters // and extend to the end of the source line. Delimited comments start with the characters /* and end with the characters */. Delimited comments may span multiple lines.

Comment:

  CommentDelimited

  CommentLine

CommentDelimited:

  /* *CommentDelimitedContents*$_{opt}$ */

CommentDelimitedContent:

  * none of /

CommentDelimitedContents:

  CommentDelimitedContent

  CommentDelimitedContents CommentDelimitedContent

CommentLine:

  // *CommentLineContents*$_{opt}$

CommentLineContent: none of

  NewLineCharacter

CommentLineContents:

  CommentLineContent

  CommentLineContents CommentLineContent

Comments do not nest. The character sequences /* and */ have no special meaning within a // comment, and the character sequences // and /* have no special meaning within a delimited comment.

Comments are not processed within text literals.

The example

```
// This defines a
// Logical literal
//
syntax LogicalLiteral
    = "true"
    | "false" ;
```

shows three single-line comments.

The example

```
/* This defines a
   Logical literal
*/
syntax LogicalLiteral
    = "true"
    | "false" ;
```

includes one delimited comment.

8.3.3 Whitespace

Whitespace is defined as any character with Unicode class Zs (which includes the space character) as well as the horizontal tab character, the vertical tab character, and the form feed character.

Whitespace:

  WhitespaceCharacters

WhitespaceCharacter:

  U+0009   *// Horizontal Tab*

  U+000B   *// Vertical Tab*

  U+000C   *// Form Feed*

  U+0020   *// Space*

NewLineCharacter

WhitespaceCharacters:

WhitespaceCharacter

WhitespaceCharacters WhitespaceCharacter

8.4 Tokens

There are several kinds of tokens: identifiers, keywords, literals, operators, and punctuators. White space and comments are not tokens, though they act as separators for tokens.

Token:

Identifier

Keyword

Literal

OperatorOrPunctuator

8.4.1 Identifiers

A regular identifier begins with a letter or underscore and then any sequence of letter, underscore, dollar sign, or digit. An escaped identifier is enclosed in square brackets. It contains any sequence of Text literal characters.

Identifier:

IdentifierBegin IdentifierCharacters$_{opt}$

IdentifierVerbatim

IdentifierBegin:

—

Letter

IdentifierCharacter:

IdentifierBegin

$

DecimalDigit

IdentifierCharacters:

   IdentifierCharacter

   IdentifierCharacters IdentifierCharacter

IdentifierVerbatim:

   [*IdentifierVerbatimCharacters*]

IdentifierVerbatimCharacter:

   none of]

   IdentifierVerbatimEscape

IdentifierVerbatimCharacters:

   IdentifierVerbatimCharacter

   IdentifierVerbatimCharacters IdentifierVerbatimCharacter

IdentifierVerbatimEscape:

   `\ \`

   `\ ]`

Letter:

   `a..z`

   `A..Z`

DecimalDigit:

   `0..9`

DecimalDigits:

   DecimalDigit

   DecimalDigits DecimalDigit

8.4.2 Keywords

A keyword is an identifier-like sequence of characters that is reserved, and cannot be used as an identifier except when escaped with square brackets [].

Keyword: oneof:

```
any empty error export false final id import interleave language labelof
left module null  precedence right syntax token true valuesof
```

The following keywords are reserved for future use:

```
checkpoint identifier nest override new virtual partial
```

8.4.3 Literals

A literal is a source code representation of a value.

Literal:

> *DecimalLiteral*
>
> *IntegerLiteral*
>
> *LogicalLiteral*
>
> *NullLiteral*
>
> *TextLiteral*

Literals may be ascribed with a type to override the default type ascription.

8.4.3.1 Decimal Literals

Decimal literals are used to write real-number values.

DecimalLiteral:

> *DecimalDigits . DecimalDigits*

Examples of decimal literal follow:

```
0.0
12.3
99999999999999.99999999999999
```

8.4.3.2 Integer Literals

Integer literals are used to write integral values.

IntegerLiteral:

  $-_{opt}$ *DecimalDigits*

Examples of integer literal follow:

```
0
123
99999999999999999999999999999
-42
```

8.4.3.3 Logical Literals

Logical literals are used to write logical values.

LogicalLiteral: one of

  true   false

Examples of logical literal:

```
true
false
```

8.4.3.4 Text Literals

M_g supports two forms of Text literals: regular text literals and verbatim text literals. In certain contexts, text literals must be of length one (single characters). However, M_g does not distinguish syntactically between strings and characters.

A regular text literal consists of zero or more characters enclosed in single or double quotes, as in "hello" or 'hello', and may include both simple escape sequences (such as \t for the tab character), and hexadecimal and Unicode escape sequences.

A verbatim Text literal consists of a "commercial at" character (@) followed by a single- or double-quote character (' or "), zero or more characters, and a closing quote character that matches the opening one. A simple example is @"hello". In a verbatim text literal, the characters between the delimiters are interpreted exactly as they occur in the compilation unit, the only exception being a *SingleQuoteEscapeSequence* or a *DoubleQuoteEscapeSequence*, depending on the opening quote. In particular, simple escape sequences, and hexadecimal and Unicode escape sequences are not processed in verbatim text literals. A verbatim text literal may span multiple lines.

A simple escape sequence represents a Unicode character encoding, as described in the following table.

Escape Sequence	Character Name	Unicode Encoding
\'	Single quote	0x0027
\"	Double quote	0x0022
\\	Backslash	0x005C
\0	Null	0x0000
\a	Alert	0x0007
\b	Backspace	0x0008
\f	Form feed	0x000C
\n	New line	0x000A
\r	Carriage return	0x000D
\t	Horizontal tab	0x0009
\v	Vertical tab	0x000B

Since M_g uses a 16-bit encoding of Unicode code points in Text values, a Unicode character in the range U+10000 to U+10FFFF is not considered a Text literal of length one (a single character), but is represented using a Unicode surrogate pair in a Text literal.

Unicode characters with code points above 0x10FFFF are not supported.

Multiple translations are not performed. For instance, the text literal \u005Cu005C is equivalent to \u005C rather than \. The Unicode value U+005C is the character \.

A hexadecimal escape sequence represents a single Unicode character, with the value formed by the hexadecimal number following the prefix.

TextLiteral:

   ' *SingleQuotedCharacters*_{opt} '

   " *DoubleQuotedCharacters*_{opt} "

   @ ' *SingleQuotedVerbatimCharacters*$_{opt}$ '

   @ " *DoubleQuotedVerbatimCharacters*$_{opt}$ "

CharacterEscape:

   CharacterEscapeHex

   CharacterEscapeSimple

   CharacterEscapeUnicode

Character:

   CharacterSimple

   CharacterEscape

Characters:

   Character

   Characters Character

CharacterEscapeHex:

   CharacterEscapeHexPrefix HexDigit

   CharacterEscapeHexPrefix HexDigit HexDigit

   CharacterEscapeHexPrefix HexDigit HexDigit HexDigit

   CharacterEscapeHexPrefix HexDigit HexDigit HexDigit HexDigit

CharacterEscapeHexPrefix: one of

   \x \X

CharacterEscapeSimple:

   \ *CharacterEscapeSimpleCharacter*

CharacterEscapeSimpleCharacter: one of

   '   "   \   0   a   b   f   n   r   t   v

CharacterEscapeUnicode:

   \u *HexDigit HexDigit HexDigit HexDigit*

   \U *HexDigit HexDigit HexDigit HexDigit HexDigit HexDigit HexDigit HexDigit*

DoubleQuotedCharacter:

   DoubleQuotedCharacterSimple

   CharacterEscape

DoubleQuotedCharacters:

   DoubleQuotedCharacter

   DoubleQuotedCharacters DoubleQuotedCharacter

DoubleQuotedCharacterSimple: none of

"

\

NewLineCharacter

SingleQuotedCharacterSimple: none of

'

\

NewLineCharacter

DoubleQuotedVerbatimCharacter:

none of "

DoubleQuotedVerbatimCharacterEscape

DoubleQuotedVerbatimCharacterEscape:

" "

DoubleQuotedVerbatimCharacters:

DoubleQuotedVerbatimCharacter

DoubleQuotedVerbatimCharacters DoubleQuotedVerbatimCharacter

SingleQuotedVerbatimCharacter:

none of "

SingleQuotedVerbatimCharacterEscape

SingleQuotedVerbatimCharacterEscape:

" "

SingleQuotedVerbatimCharacters:

SingleQuotedVerbatimCharacter

SingleQuotedVerbatimCharacters SingleQuotedVerbatimCharacter

Examples of text literals follow:

```
'a'
'\u2323'
'\x2323'
'2323'
"Hello World"
@"""Hello,
World"""
"\u2323"
```

8.4.3.5 Null Literal

The null literal is equal to no other value.

NullLiteral:

```
null
```

An example of the null literal follows:

```
null
```

8.4.4 Operators and Punctuators

There are several kinds of operators and punctuators. Operators are used in expressions to describe operations involving one or more operands. For example, the expression `a + b` uses the `+` operator to add the two operands `a` and `b`. Punctuators are for grouping and separating.

OperatorOrPunctuator: one of

```
[ ]   ( )   .   ,   :   ;   ?   =   =>   +   -   *   &   |   ^   { }   #   ..   @   '   "
```

8.5 Pre-processing Directives

Pre-processing directives provide the ability to conditionally skip sections of source files, to report error and warning conditions, and to delineate distinct regions of source code as a separate pre-processing step.

PPDirective:

 PPDeclaration

 PPConditional

 PPDiagnostic

 PPRegion

The following pre-processing directives are available:

- `#define` and `#undef`, which are used to define and undefine, respectively, conditional compilation symbols.
- `#if`, `#else`, and `#endif`, which are used to conditionally skip sections of source code.

A pre-processing directive always occupies a separate line of source code and always begins with a `#` character and a pre-processing directive name. White space may occur before the `#` character and between the `#` character and the directive name.

A source line containing a `#define`, `#undef`, `#if`, `#else`, or `#endif` directive may end with a single-line comment. Delimited comments (the `/* */` style of comments) are not permitted on source lines containing pre-processing directives.

Pre-processing directives are neither tokens nor part of the syntactic grammar of M_g. However, pre-processing directives can be used to include or exclude sequences of tokens and can in that way affect the meaning of an M_g program. For example, after pre-processing the source text:

```
#define A
#undef B
language C
{
#if A
    syntax F = "ABC";
#else
    syntax G = "HIJ";
#endif
#if B
    syntax H = "KLM";
#else
    syntax I = "DEF";
#endif
}
```

results in the exact same sequence of tokens as the source text:

```
language C
{
    syntax F = "ABC";
    syntax I = "DEF";
}
```

Thus, whereas lexically the two programs are quite different, syntactically they are identical.

8.5.1 Conditional Compilation Symbols

The conditional compilation functionality provided by the `#if`, `#else`, and `#endif` directives is controlled through pre-processing expressions and conditional compilation symbols.

ConditionalSymbol:

> Any *IdentifierOrKeyword* except `true` or `false`

A conditional compilation symbol has two possible states: defined or undefined. At the beginning of the lexical processing of a source file, a conditional compilation symbol is undefined unless it has been explicitly defined by an external mechanism (such as a command-line compiler option). When a `#define` directive is processed, the conditional compilation symbol named in that directive becomes defined in that source file. The symbol remains defined until an `#undef` directive for that same symbol is processed, or until the end of the source file is reached. An implication of this is that `#define` and `#undef` directives in one source file have no effect on other source files in the same program.

When referenced in a pre-processing expression, a defined conditional compilation symbol has the Logical value `true`, and an undefined conditional compilation symbol has the Logical value `false`. There is no requirement that conditional compilation symbols be explicitly declared before they are referenced in pre-processing expressions. Instead, undeclared symbols are simply undefined and thus have the value `false`.

Conditional compilation symbols can only be referenced in `#define` and `#undef` directives and in pre-processing expressions.

8.5.2 Pre-processing Expressions

Pre-processing expressions can occur in `#if` directives. The operators `!`, `==`, `!=`, `&&`, and `||` are permitted in pre-processing expressions, and parentheses may be used for grouping.

PPExpression:

> *Whitespace*$_{opt}$ *PPOrExpression*   *Whitespace*$_{opt}$

OrExpression:

   PPAndExpression

   PPOrExpression Whitespace$_{opt}$ || *Whitespace$_{opt}$ PPAndExpression*

PPAndExpression:

   PPEqualityExpression

   PPAndExpression Whitespace$_{opt}$ && *Whitespace$_{opt}$ PPEqualityExpression*

PPEqualityExpression:

   PPUnaryExpression

   PPEqualityExpression Whitespace$_{opt}$ == *Whitespace$_{opt}$ PPUnaryExpression*

   PPEqualityExpression Whitespace$_{opt}$!= *Whitespace$_{opt}$ PPUnaryExpression*

PPUnaryExpression:

   PPPrimaryExpression

   ! *Whitespace$_{opt}$ PPUnaryExpression*

PPPrimaryExpression:

   `true`

   `false`

   ConditionalSymbol

   (*Whitespace$_{opt}$ PPExpression Whitespace$_{opt}$*)

When referenced in a pre-processing expression, a defined conditional compilation symbol has the Logical value `true`, and an undefined conditional compilation symbol has the Logical value `false`.

Evaluation of a pre-processing expression always yields a Logical value. The rules of evaluation for a pre-processing expression are the same as those for a constant expression, except that the only user-defined entities that can be referenced are conditional compilation symbols.

8.5.3 Declaration Directives

The declaration directives are used to define or undefine conditional compilation symbols.

PPDeclaration:

   *Whitespace*_{opt} # *Whitespace*_{opt} define *Whitespace* *ConditionalSymbol* *PPNewLine*

   *Whitespace*_{opt} # *Whitespace*_{opt} undef *Whitespace* *ConditionalSymbol* *PPNewLine*

PPNewLine:

   *Whitespace*_{opt} *SingleLineComment*_{opt} *NewLine*

The processing of a `#define` directive causes the given conditional compilation symbol to become defined, starting with the source line that follows the directive. Likewise, the processing of an `#undef` directive causes the given conditional compilation symbol to become undefined, starting with the source line that follows the directive.

A `#define` may define a conditional compilation symbol that is already defined, without there being any intervening `#undef` for that symbol. The following example defines a conditional compilation symbol A and then defines it again.

```
#define A
#define A
```

A `#undef` may "undefine" a conditional compilation symbol that is not defined. The following example defines a conditional compilation symbol A and then undefines it twice; although the second `#undef` has no effect, it is still valid.

```
#define A
#undef A
#undef A
```

8.5.4 Conditional Compilation Directives

The conditional compilation directives are used to conditionally include or exclude portions of a source file.

PPConditional:

   PPIfSection *PPElseSection*_{opt} *PPEndif*

PPIfSection:

   *Whitespace*_{opt} # *Whitespace*_{opt} if *Whitespace* *PPExpression* *PPNewLine* *ConditionalSection*_{opt}

PPElseSection:

    Whitespace$_{opt}$ # *Whitespace*$_{opt}$ else *PPNewLine ConditionalSection*$_{opt}$

PPEndif:

    Whitespace$_{opt}$ # *Whitespace*$_{opt}$ endif *PPNewLine*

ConditionalSection:

    InputSection

    SkippedSection

SkippedSection:

    SkippedSectionPart

    SkippedSection   SkippedSectionPart

SkippedSectionPart:

    SkippedCharacters$_{opt}$ *NewLine*

    PPDirective

SkippedCharacters:

    Whitespace$_{opt}$ *NotNumberSign InputCharacters*$_{opt}$

NotNumberSign:

    Any *InputCharacter* except #

As indicated by the syntax, conditional compilation directives must be written as sets consisting of, in order, an #if directive, zero or one #else directive, and an #endif directive. Between the directives are conditional sections of source code. Each section is controlled by the immediately preceding directive. A conditional section may itself contain nested conditional compilation directives provided these directives form complete sets.

A *PPConditional* selects at most one of the contained *ConditionalSection*s for normal lexical processing:

- The *PPExpressions* of the #if directives are evaluated in order until one yields true. If an expression yields true, the *ConditionalSection* of the corresponding directive is selected.
- If all *PPExpressions* yield false, and if an #else directive is present, the *ConditionalSection* of the #else directive is selected.
- Otherwise, no *ConditionalSection* is selected.

The selected *ConditionalSection*, if any, is processed as a normal *InputSection*: the source code contained in the section must adhere to the lexical grammar; tokens are generated from the source code in the section; and pre-processing directives in the section have the prescribed effects.

The remaining *ConditionalSection*s, if any, are processed as *SkippedSection*s: except for pre-processing directives, the source code in the section need not adhere to the lexical grammar; no tokens are generated from the source code in the section; and pre-processing directives in the section must be lexically correct but are not otherwise processed. Within a *ConditionalSection* that is being processed as a *SkippedSection*, any nested *ConditionalSection*s (contained in nested `#if...#endif` and `#region...#endregion` constructs) are also processed as *SkippedSection*s.

Except for pre-processing directives, skipped source code is not subject to lexical analysis. For example, the following is valid despite the unterminated comment in the `#else` section:

```
#define Debug          // Debugging on
module HelloWorld {
    language HelloWorld {
        syntax Main =
#if Debug
            "Hello World"
        ;
#else
        /* Unterminated comment!
#endif
    }
}
```

Note that pre-processing directives are required to be lexically correct even in skipped sections of source code.

Pre-processing directives are not processed when they appear inside multi-line input elements. For example, the program:

```
module HelloWorld {
    language HelloWorld {
        syntax Main = @'
#if Debug
            "Hello World"
        ;
```

```
#else
        /* Unterminated comment!
#endif'
    }
}
```

generates a language which recognizes the value:

```
#if Debug
        "Hello World"
        ;
#else
        /* Unterminated comment!
#endif
```

In peculiar cases, the set of pre-processing directives that is processed might depend on the evaluation of the *PPExpression*. The example:

```
#if X
    /*
#else
    /* */ syntax Q = empty;
#endif
```

always produces the same token stream (`syntax Q = empty;`) regardless of whether or not x is defined. If x is defined, the only processed directives are `#if` and `#endif`, due to the multi-line comment. If x is undefined, then three directives (`#if`, `#else`, `#endif`) are part of the directive set.

CHAPTER 9

TEXT PATTERN EXPRESSIONS

Text pattern expressions perform operations on the sets of possible text values that one or more terms recognize.

9.1 Primary Expressions

A primary expression can be:

- A text literal
- A reference to a syntax or token rule
- An expression indicating a repeated sequence of primary expressions of a specified length
- An expression indicating any of a continuous range of characters
- An inline sequence of pattern declarations

The following grammar reflects this structure.

Primary:

    ReferencePrimary

    TextLiteral

    RepetitionPrimary

    CharacterClassPrimary

    InlineRulePrimary

    AnyPrimary

9.1.1 Character Class

A character class is a compact syntax for a range of continuous characters. This expression requires that the text literals be of length 1 and that the Unicode offset of the right operand be greater than that of the left.

CharacterClassPrimary:

   TextLiteral .. *TextLiteral*

The expression `"0".."9"` is equivalent to:

`"0" | "1" | "2" | "3" | "4" | "5" | "6" | "7" | "8" | "9"`

9.1.2 References

A reference primary is the name of another rule possibly with arguments for parameterized rules. All rules defined within the same language can be accessed without qualification. The protocol to access rules defined in a different language within the same module are defined in Section 12.2. The protocol to access rules defined in a different module are defined in Section 13.3.

ReferencePrimary:

   GrammarReference

GrammarReference:

   Identifier

   GrammarReference . *Identifier*

   GrammarReference . *Identifier* (*TypeArguments*)

   Identifier (*TypeArguments*)

TypeArguments:

   PrimaryExpression

   TypeArguments , *PrimaryExpression*

Note that whitespace between a rule name and its arguments list is significant to discriminate between a reference to a parameterized rule and a reference without parameters and an inline rule. In a reference to a parameterized rule, no whitespace is permitted between the identifier and the arguments.

9.1.3 Repetition Operators

The repetition operators recognize a primary expression repeated a specified number of times. The number of repetitions can be stated as a (possibly open) integer range or using one of the Kleene operators, `?`, `+`, `*`.

RepetitionPrimary:

   Primary Range

   Primary CollectionRanges

Range:

   ?

   *

   +

CollectionRanges:

   # *IntegerLiteral*

   # *IntegerLiteral* .. *IntegerLiteral*_{opt}

The left operand of `..` must be greater than zero and less than the right operand of `..`, if present.

`"A"#5`	recognizes exactly 5 `"A"`s	`"AAAAA"`
`"A"#2..4`	recognizes from 2 to 4 `"A"`s	`"AA"`, `"AAA"`, `"AAAA"`
`"A"#3..`	recognizes 3 or more `"A"`s	`"AAA"`, `"AAAA"`, `"AAAAA"`, . . .

The Kleene operators can be defined in terms of the collection range operator:

   `"A"?` is equivalent to `"A"#0..1`
   `"A"+` is equivalent to `"A"#1..`
   `"A"*` is equivalent to `"A"#0..`

9.1.4 Inline Rules

An inline rule is a means to group pattern declarations together as a term.

InlineRulePrimary:

(*ProductionDeclarations*)

An inline rule is typically used in conjunction with a range operator:

"A" ("," "A")* recognizes 1 or more "A"s separated by commas.

Although syntactically legal, variable bindings within inline rules are not accessible within the constructor of the containing production. Inline rules are described further in Section 11.4.

9.1.5 Any

The any term is a wildcard that matches any text value of length 1.

Any:

any

"1", "z", and "*" all match any.

9.1.6 Error

The error production enables error recovery. Consider the following example:

```
module HelloWorld {
    language HelloWorld {
        syntax Main
          = HelloList;
        token Hello
          = "Hello";
        checkpoint syntax HelloList
          = Hello
          | HelloList "," Hello
          | HelloList "," error;
    }
}
```

The language recognizes the text `"Hello,Hello,Hello"` as expected and produces the following default output:

```
Main[
  HelloList[
    HelloList[
      HelloList[
        Hello
      ],
      ,,
      Hello
    ],
    ,,
    Hello
  ]
]
```

The text `"Hello,hello,Hello"` is not in the language because the second `"h"` is not capitalized (and case sensitivity is true). However, rather than stop at `"h"`, the language processor matches `"h"` to the `error` token, then matches `"e"` to the `error` token, and so forth. Until it reaches the comma. At this point the text conforms to the language and normal processing can continue. The language process reports the position of the errors and produces the following output:

```
Main[
  HelloList[
    HelloList[
      HelloList[
        Hello
      ],
      error["hello"],
    ],
    ,,
    Hello
  ]
]
```

`Hello` occurs twice instead of three times as above and the text the `error` token matched is returned as `error["hello"]`.

9.2 Term Operators

A primary term expression can be thought of as the set of possible text values that it recognizes. The term operators perform the standard set difference, intersection, and negation operations on these sets. (Pattern declarations perform the union operation with |.)

TextPatternExpression:

   Difference

Difference:

   Intersect

   Difference - Intersect

Intersect:

   Inverse

   Intersect & Inverse

Inverse:

   Primary

   ^ Primary

Inverse requires every value in the set of possible text values to be of length 1.

   `("11" | "12") - ("12" | "13")` recognizes `"11"`.

   `("11" | "12") & ("12" | "13")` recognizes `"12"`.

   `^("11" | "12")` is an error.

   `^("1" | "2")` recognizes any text value of length 1 other than `"1"` or `"2"`.

CHAPTER 10

PRODUCTIONS

A production is a pattern and an optional constructor. Each production is a scope. The pattern may establish variable bindings which can be referenced in the constructor. A production can be qualified with a precedence that is used to resolve a tie if two productions match the same text (see Section 10.4.1).

ProductionDeclaration:

    *ProductionPrecedence*_{opt} → $ProductionPrecedence_{opt}$ *PatternDeclaration Constructor*_{opt}

Constructor

    `=>` *TermConstructor*

ProductionPrecedence:

    `precedence` *IntegerLiteral* `:`

10.1 Pattern Declaration

A pattern declaration is a sequence of term declarations or the built-in pattern `empty` which matches `""`.

PatternDeclaration:

    empty

    *TermDeclarations*_{opt}

TermDeclarations:

    TermDeclaration

    TermDeclarations TermDeclaration

10.2 Term Declaration

A term declaration consists of a pattern expression with an optional variable binding, precedence and attributes. The built-in term error is used for error recovery and discussed in Section 9.1.6.

TermDeclaration:

   error

   Attributes$_{opt}$ TermPrecedence$_{opt}$ VariableBinding$_{opt}$ TextPatternExpression

VariableBinding:

   Name :

TermPrecedence:

   left (*IntegerLiteral*)

   right (*IntegerLiteral*)

A variable associates a name with the output from a term which can be used in the constructor. Precedence is discussed in Section 10.4.2.

   The error term is used in conjunction with the checkpoint rule modifier to facilitate error recovery. This is described in Section 9.1.6.

10.3 Constructors

A term constructor is the syntax for defining the output of a production. A node in a term constructor can be:

- An atom consisting of
  - A literal
  - A reference to another term
  - An operation on a reference
- An ordered collection of successors with an optional label
- An unordered collection of successors with an optional label

The following grammar mirrors this structure.

TermConstructor:

   TopLevelNode

Node:

   Atom

   OrderedTerm

   UnorderedTerm

TopLevelNode:

   TopLevelAtom

   OrderedTerm

   UnorderedTerm

Nodes:

   Node

   Nodes , Node

OrderedTerm:

   Label$_{opt}$ [*Nodes*$_{opt}$]

UnorderedTerm:

   Label$_{opt}$ { *Nodes*$_{opt}$ }

Label:

   Identifier

   `id` (*Atom*)

Atom:

   TopLevelAtom

   `valuesof` (*VariableReference*)

TopLevelAtom:

   TextLiteral

   DecimalLiteral

   LogicalLiteral

IntegerLiteral

NullLiteral

VariableReference

labelof (*VariableReference*)

VariableReference:

Identifier

Each production defines a scope. The variables referenced in a constructor must be defined within the same production's pattern. Variables defined in other productions in the same rule cannot be referenced. The same variable name can be used across alternatives in the same rule.

Consider three alternatives for encoding the output of the same production. First, the default constructor (see Section 10.3.2):

```
module Expression {
    language Expression {
        token Digits = ("0".."9")+;
        syntax Main = E;
        syntax E
          = Digits
          | E "+" E ;
    }
}
```

Processing the text `"1+2"` yields:

```
Main[E[E[1], +, E[2]]]
```

This output reflects the structure of the grammar and may not be the most useful form for further processing. The second alternative cleans the output up considerably:

```
module Expression {
    language Expression {
        token Digits = ("0".."9")+;
        syntax Main
          = e:E => e;
        syntax E
```

```
            = d:Digits => d
            | l:E "+" r:E => Add[l,r] ;
    }
}
```

Processing the text `"1+2"` with this language yields:

```
Add[1, 2]
```

This grammar uses three common patterns:

- Productions with a single term are passed through. This is done for the single production in `Main` and the first production in `E`.
- A label, `Add`, is used to designate the operator.
- Position is used to distinguish the left and right operand.

The third alternative uses a record like structure to give the operands names:

```
module Expression {
    language Expression {
        token Digits = ("0".."9")+;
        syntax Main
          = e:E => e;
        syntax E
          = d:Digits => d
          | l:E "+" r:E => Add{Left{l},Right{r}} ;
    }
}
```

Processing the text `"1+2"` with this language yields:

```
Add{Left{1}, Right{2}}
```

Although somewhat more verbose than the prior alternative, this output does not rely on ordering and forces consumers to explicitly name `Left` or `Right` operands. Although either option works, this has proven to be more flexible and less error prone.

10.3.1 Constructor Operators

Constructor operators allow a constructor to use a variable reference as a label, extract the successors of a variable reference, or extract the label of a variable reference.

Consider generalizing the previous example to support multiple operators. This could be done by adding a new production for each operator -, *, /, ^. Alternatively a single rule can be established to match these operators and the output of that rule can be used as a label using id:

```
module Expression {
    language Expression {
        token Digits = ("0".."9")+;
        syntax Main
          = e:E => e;
        syntax Op
          = "+" => "Add"
          | "-" => "Subtract"
          | "*" => "Multiply"
          | "/" => "Divide" ;
        syntax E
          = d:Digits => d
          | l:E o:Op r:E => id(o){Left[l],Right[r]} ;
    }
}
```

Processing the text `"1+2"` with this language yields the same result as above. Processing `"1 / 2"` yields:

```
Divide{Left{1}, Right{2}}
```

This language illustrates the id operator. See Section 10.4.2 for a more realistic expression grammar.

The valuesof operator extracts the successors of a variable reference. It is used to flatten nested output structures. Consider the language:

```
module Digits {
    language Digits {
        syntax Main = DigitList ;
        token Digit = "0".."9";
```

```
            syntax DigitList
              = Digit
              | DigitList "," Digit ;
        }
}
```

Processing the text `"1, 2, 3"` with this language yields:

```
Main[
  DigitList[
    DigitList[
      DigitList[
        1
      ],
      ','
      2
    ],
    ','
    3
  ]
]
```

The following grammar uses `valuesof` and the pass through pattern above to simplify the output:

```
module Digits {
    language Digits {
        syntax Main = dl:DigitList => dl ;
        token Digit = "0".."9";
        syntax DigitList
          = d:Digit => DigitList[d]
          | dl:DigitList "," d:Digit => DigitList[valuesof(dl),d] ;
    }
}
```

Processing the text `"1, 2, 3"` with this language yields:

```
DigitList[1, 2, 3]
```

This output represents the same information more concisely.

10.3.2 Default Constructor

If a constructor is not defined for a production, the language process defines a default constructor. For a given production, the default projection is formed as follows:

1. The label for the result is the name of the production's rule.
2. The successors of the result are an ordered sequence constructed from each term in the pattern.
3. * and ? create an unlabeled sequence with the elements.
4. ( ) results in an anonymous definition.
    a. If it contains constructors (a:A => a), then the output is the output of the constructor.
    b. If there are no constructors, then the default rule applied on the anonymous definition and the output is enclosed in square brackets [A's result]
5. Token rules do not permit a constructor to be specified and output text values.
6. Interleave rules do not permit a constructor to be specified and do not produce output.

Consider the following language:

```
module ThreeDigits {
    language ThreeDigits {
        token Digit = "0".."9";
        syntax Main
          = Digit Digit Digit ;
    }
}
```

Given the text "123" the default output of the language processor follows:

```
Main[
    1,
    2,
    3
]
```

10.4 Precedence

The M_g language processor is tolerant of such ambiguity as it is recognizing subsequences of text. However, it is an error to produce more than one output for an entire text value. Precedence qualifiers on productions or terms determine which of the several outputs should be returned.

10.4.1 Production Precedence

Consider the classic dangling else problem as represented in the following language:

```
module IfThenElse {
    language IfThenElse {
        syntax Main = S;
        syntax S
          = empty
          | "if" E "then" S
          | "if" E "then" S "else" S;
        syntax E = empty;
        interleave Whitespace_ = " ";
    }
}
```

Given the input "if then if then else", two different output are possible. Either the else binds to the first if-then:

```
if
then
    if
    then
else
```

Or it binds to the second if-then:

```
if
then
    if
    then
    else
```

The following language produces the output immediately above, binding the else to the second if-then.

```
module IfThenElse {
    language IfThenElse {
        syntax Main = S;
        syntax S
          = empty
          | precedence 2: "if" E "then" S
          | precedence 1: "if" E "then" S "else" S;
        syntax E = empty;
        interleave Whitespace = " ";
    }
}
```

Switching the precedence values produces the first output.

10.4.2 Term Precedence

Consider a simple expression language which recognizes:

```
2 + 3 + 4
5 * 6 * 7
2 + 3 * 4
2 ^ 3 ^ 4
```

The result of these expressions can depend on the order in which the operators are reduced. 2 + 3 + 4 yields 9 whether 2 + 3 is evaluated first or 3 + 4 is evaluated first. Likewise, 5 * 6 * 7 yields 210 regardless of the order of evaluation.

However, this is not the case for 2 + 3 * 4. If 2 + 3 is evaluated first yielding 5, then 5 * 4 yields 20. While if 3 * 4 is evaluated first yielding 12, then 2 + 12 yields 14. This difference manifests itself in the output of the following grammar:

```
module Expression {
    language Expression {
        token Digits = ("0".."9")+;
        syntax Main = e:E => e;
        syntax E
          = d:Digits => d
          | "(" e:E ")" => e
```

```
        | l:E "^" r:E => Exp[l,r]
        | l:E "*" r:E => Mult[l,r]
        | l:E "+" r:E => Add[l,r];
      interleave Whitespace = " ";
    }
}
```

`"2 + 3 * 4"` can result in two outputs:

```
Mult[Add[2, 3], 4]
Add[2, Mult[3, 4]]
```

According to the rules we all learned in school, the result of this expression is 14 because multiplication is performed before addition. This is expressed in M_g by assigning `"*"` a higher precedence than `"+"`. In this case the result of an expression changed with the order of evaluation of different operators.

The order of evaluation of a single operator can matter as well. Consider 2 ^ 3 ^ 4. This could result in either 8 ^ 4 or 2 ^ 81. In term of output, there are two possibilities:

```
Exp[Exp[2, 3], 4]
Exp[2, Exp[3, 4]]
```

In this case the issue is not which of several different operators to evaluate first but which in a sequence of operators to evaluate first, the leftmost or the rightmost. The rule in this case is less well established but most languages choose to evaluate the rightmost `"^"` first yielding 2 ^ 81 in this example.

The following grammar implements these rules using term precedence qualifiers. Term precedence qualifiers may only be applied to literals or references to token rules.

```
module Expression {
    language Expression {
        token Digits = ("0".."9")+;
        syntax Main = E;
        syntax E
          = d:Digits => d
          | "(" e:E ")" => e
          | l:E right(3) "^" r:E => Exp[l,r]
          | l:E left(2) "*" r:E => Mult[l,r]
```

```
        | l:E left(1) "+" r:E => Add[l,r];
      interleave Whitespace = " ";
   }
}
```

"`^`" is qualified with `right(3)`. `right` indicates that the rightmost in a sequence should be grouped together first. 3 is the highest precedence, so "`^`" will be grouped most strongly.

CHAPTER 11

RULES

A rule is a named collection of alternative productions. There are three kinds of rules: `syntax`, `token`, and `interleave`. A text value conforms to a rule if it conforms to any one of the productions in the rule. If a text value conforms to more than one production in the rule, then the rule is ambiguous. The three different kinds of rules differ in how they treat ambiguity and how they handle their output.

RuleDeclaration:

    Attributes$_{opt}$ MemberModifiers$_{opt}$ Kind Name RuleParameters$_{opt}$ RuleBody$_{opt}$;

Kind:

    token

    syntax

    interleave

MemberModifiers:

    MemberModifier

    MemberModifiers MemberModifer

MemberModifier:

    final

    identifier

RuleBody:

    = ProductionDeclarations

ProductionDeclarations:

    ProductionDeclaration

    ProductionDeclarations | ProductionDeclaration

The rule `Main` below recognizes the two text values `"Hello"` and `"Goodbye"`.

```
module HelloGoodby {
    language HelloGoodbye {
        syntax Main
          = "Hello"
          | "Goodbye"; .
    }
}
```

11.1 Token Rules

Token rules recognize a restricted family of languages. However, token rules can be negated, intersected, and subtracted, which is not the case for syntax rules. Attempting to perform these operations on a syntax rule results in an error. The output from a token rule is the text matched by the token. No constructor may be defined.

11.1.1 Final Modifier

Token rules do not permit precedence directives in the rule body. They have a built-in protocol to deal with ambiguous productions. A language processor attempts to match all tokens in the language against a text value starting with the first character, then the first two, etc. If two or more productions within the same token or two different tokens can match the beginning of a text value, a token rule will choose the production with the longest match. If all matches are exactly the same length, the language processor will choose a token rule marked `final` if present. If no token rule is marked `final`, all the matches succeed and the language processor evaluates whether each alternative is recognized in a larger context. The language processor retains all of the matches and begins attempting to match a new token starting with the first character that has not already been matched.

11.1.2 Identifier Modifier

The identifier modifier applies only to tokens. It is used to lower the precedence of language identifiers so they do not conflict with language keywords.

11.2 Syntax Rules

Syntax rules recognize all languages that M_g is capable of defining. The `Main` start rule must be a syntax rule. Syntax rules allow all precedence directives and may have constructors.

11.3 Interleave Rules

An interleave rule recognizes the same family of languages as a token rule and also cannot have constructors. Further, interleave rules cannot have parameters and the name of an interleave rule cannot be references.

Text that matches an interleave rule is excluded from further processing.

The following example demonstrates whitespace handling with an interleave rule:

```
module HelloWorld {
    language HelloWorld {
        syntax Main =
          = Hello World;
        token Hello
          = "Hello";
        token World
          = "World";
        interleave Whitespace
          = " ";
    }
}
```

This language recognizes the text value `"Hello World"`. It also recognizes `"Hello World"`, `"   Hello World"`, `"Hello World   "`, and `"HelloWorld"`. It does not recognize `"He llo World"` because `"He"` does not match any token.

11.4 Inline Rules

An inline rule is an anonymous rule embedded within the pattern of a production. The inline rule is processed as any other rule; however, it cannot be reused since it does not have a name. Variables defined within an inline rule are scoped to their productions as usual. A variable may be bound to the output of an inline rule as with any pattern.

In the following, `Example1` and `Example2` recognize the same language and produce the same output. `Example1` uses a named rule `AppleOrOrange` while `Example2` states the same rule inline.

```
module Example {
    language Example1 {
        syntax Main
            = aos:AppleOrOrange*
                => aos;

        syntax AppleOrOrange
            = "Apple" => Apple{}
            | "Orange" => Orange{};
    }

    language Example2 {
        syntax Main
            = aos:("Apple" => Apple{} | "Orange" => Orange{})*
                => aos;
    }
}
```

11.5 Rule Parameters

A rule may define parameters that can be used within the body of the rule.

RuleParameters:

  (*RuleParameterList*)

RuleParameterList:

  RuleParameter

  RuleParameterList , *RuleParameter*

RuleParameter:

  Identifier

A single rule identifier may have multiple definitions with different numbers of parameters. The following example uses `List(Content,Separator)` to define `List(Content)` with a default separator of `","`.

```
module HelloWorld {
    language HelloWorld {
        syntax Main
          = List(Hello);
        token Hello
          = "Hello";
        syntax List(Content, Separator)
          = Content
          | List(Content,Separator) Separator Content;

        syntax List(Content) = List(Content, ",");
    }
}
```

This language will recognize `"Hello"`, `"Hello,Hello"`, `"Hello,Hello,Hello"`, and so on.

CHAPTER 12

LANGUAGES

A language is a named collection of rules for imposing structure on text.

LanguageDeclaration:

   Attributes$_{opt}$ language *Name LanguageBody*

LanguageBody:

   { *RuleDeclarations*$_{opt}$ }

RuleDeclarations:

   RuleDeclaration

   RuleDeclarations RuleDeclaration

The language that follows recognizes the single text value `"Hello World"`:

```
module HelloWorld {
    language HelloWorld {
        syntax Main
            = "Hello World";
    }
}
```

12.1 Main Rule

A language may consist of any number of rules. The following language recognizes the single text value `"Hello World"`:

```
module HelloWorld {
    language HelloWorld {
        syntax Main
            = Hello Whitespace World;
        token Hello
            = "Hello";
```

```
      token World
        = "World";
      token Whitespace
        = " ";
    }
}
```

The three rules `Hello`, `World`, and `Whitespace` recognize the three single text values `"Hello"`, `"World"`, and `" "` respectively. The rule `Main` combines these three rules in sequence. The difference between syntax and token rules is described in Section 11.1.

   `Main` is the distinguished start rule for a language. A language recognizes a text value if and only if `Main` recognizes a value. Also, the output for `Main` is the output for the language.

12.2 Cross-Language Rule References

Rules are members of a language. A language can use rules defined in another language using member access notation. The `HelloWorld` language recognizes the single text value `"Hello World"` using rules defined in the `Words` language:

```
module HelloWorld {

    language Words {
        token Hello
          = "Hello";
        token World
          = "World";
    }

    language HelloWorld {
        syntax Main
          = Words.Hello Whitespace Words.World;
        token Whitespace =
          = " ";
    }
}
```

All rules defined within the same module are accessible in this way. Rules defined in other modules must be exported and imported as defined in the next chapter.

CHAPTER 13

MODULES

An M_g module is a scope that contains declarations of languages (Chapter 12). Declarations exported by an imported module are made available in the importing module. Thus, modules override lexical scoping that otherwise governs M_g symbol resolution. Modules themselves do not nest.

13.1 Compilation Unit

Several modules may be contained within a *CompilationUnit*, typically a text file.

CompilationUnit:

    ModuleDeclarations

ModuleDeclarations:

    ModuleDeclaration

    ModuleDeclarations ModuleDeclaration

13.2 Module Declaration

A *ModuleDeclaration* is a named container/scope for language declarations.

ModuleDeclaration:

    `module` *QualifiedIdentifer ModuleBody* ;$_{opt}$

QualifiedIdentifier:

    Identifier

QualifiedIdentifier . Identifier

ModuleBody:

   { *ImportDirectives ExportDirectives ModuleMemberDeclarations* }

ModuleMemberDeclarations:

   ModuleMemberDeclaration

   ModuleMemberDeclarations ModuleMemberDeclaration

ModuleMemberDeclaration:

   LanguageDeclaration

Each *ModuleDeclaration* has a *QualifiedIdentifier* that uniquely qualifies the declarations contained by the module.

Each *ModuleMemberDeclaration* may be referenced either by its *Identifier* or by its fully qualified name by concatenating the *QualifiedIdentifier* of the *ModuleDeclaration* with the *Identifier* of the *ModuleMemberDeclaration* (separated by a period).

For example, given the following *ModuleDeclaration*:

```
module BaseDefinitions {
    export Logical;
    language Logical {
        syntax Literal = "true" | "false";
    }
}
```

The fully qualified name of the language is `BaseDefinitions.Logical`, or using escaped identifiers, `[BaseDefinitions].[Logical]`. It is always legal to use a fully qualified name where the name of a declaration is expected.

Modules are not hierarchical or nested. That is, there is no implied relationship between modules whose *QualifiedIdentifier* share a common prefix.

For example, consider these two declarations:

```
module A {
    language L {
        token I = ('0'..'9')+;
    }
}
module A.B {
```

```
language M {
    token D = L.I '.' L.I;
}
}
```

Module A.B is in error, as it does not contain a declaration for the identifier L. That is, the members of Module A are not implicitly imported into Module A.B.

13.3 Inter-Module Dependencies

M_g uses *ImportDirectives* and *ExportDirectives* to explicitly control which declarations may be used across module boundaries.

ExportDirectives:

    ExportDirective

    ExportDirectives ExportDirective

ExportDirective:

    export *Identifiers* ;

ImportDirectives:

    ImportDirective

    ImportDirectives ImportDirective

ImportDirective:

    import *ImportModules* ;

    import *QualifiedIdentifier* { *ImportMembers* } ;

ImportMember:

    Identifier ImportAlias$_{opt}$

ImportMembers:

    ImportMember

    ImportMembers , ImportMember

ImportModule:

    QualifiedIdentifier ImportAlias$_{opt}$

ImportModules:

    ImportModule

ImportModules , *ImportModule*

ImportAlias:

  as *Identifier*

A *ModuleDeclaration* contains zero or more *ExportDirectives*, each of which makes a *ModuleMemberDeclaration* available to declarations outside of the current module.

A *ModuleDeclaration* contains zero or more *ImportDirectives*, each of which names a *ModuleDeclaration* whose declarations may be referenced by the current module.

A *ModuleMemberDeclaration* may only reference declarations in the current module and declarations that have an explicit *ImportDirective* in the current module.

An *ImportDirective* is not transitive, that is, importing module *A* does not import the modules that *A* imports.

For example, consider this *ModuleDeclaration*:

```
module Language.Core {
    export Base;

    language Internal {
        token Digit = '0'..'9';
        token Letter = 'A'..'Z' | 'a'..'z';
    }

    language Base {
        token Identifier = Letter (Letter | Digit)*;
    }
}
```

The definition `Language.Core.Internal` may be referenced only from within the module `Language.Core`. The definition `Language.Core.Base` may be referenced in any module that has an *ImportDirective* for module `Language.Core`, as shown in this example:

```
module Language.Extensions {
    import Language.Core;
```

```
    language Names {
        syntax QualifiedIdentifier
            = Language.Core.Base.Identifier '.'
Language.Core.Base.Identifier;
    }
}
```

The preceding example uses the fully qualified name to refer to `Language.Core.Base`. An *ImportDirective* may also specify an *ImportAlias* that provides a replacement *Identifier* for the imported declaration:

```
module Language.Extensions {
    import Language.Core as lc;

    language Names {
        syntax QualifiedIdentifier
            = lc.Base.Identifier '.' lc.Base.Identifier;
    }
}
```

An *ImportAlias* replaces the name of the imported declaration. This means that the following is an error:

```
module Language.Extensions {
    import Language.Core as lc;

    language Names {
        syntax QualifiedIdentifier
            = Language.Core.Base.Identifier '.'
Language.Core.Base.Identifier;
    }
}
```

It is legal for two or more *ImportDirectives* to import the same declaration, provided they specify distinct aliases. For a given compilation episode, at most one *ImportDirective* may use a given alias.

If an *ImportDirective* imports a module without specifying an alias, the declarations in the imported module may be referenced without the qualification of the module name.

That means the following is also legal.

```
module Language.Extensions {
    import Language.Core;

    language Names {
        syntax QualifiedIdentifier = Base.Identifier '.' Base.Identifier;
    }
}
```

When two modules contain same-named declarations, there is a potential for ambiguity. The potential for ambiguity is not an error—ambiguity errors are detected lazily as part of resolving references.

Consider the following two modules:

```
module A {
    export L;
    language L {
        token X = '1';
    }
}
module B {
    export L;
    language L {
        token X = '2';
    }
}
```

It is legal to import both modules either with or without providing an alias:

```
module C {
    import A, B;
    language M {
        token Y = '3';
    }
}
```

This is legal because ambiguity is only an error for references, not declarations. This means that the following is a compile-time error:

```
module C {
    import A, B;
    language M {
        token Y = L.X | '3';
    }
}
```

This example can be made legal either by fully qualifying the reference to L:

```
module C {
    import A, B;
    language M {
        token Y = A.L.X | '3';    // no error
    }
}
```

or by adding an alias to one or both of the *ImportDirective*s:

```
module C {
    import A;
    import B as bb;
    language M {
        token Y = L.X | '3';    // no error, refers to A.L
        token Z = bb.L.X | '3';    // no error, refers to B.L
    }
}
```

An *ImportDirective* may either import all exported declarations from a module or only a selected subset of them. The latter is enabled by specifying *ImportMembers* as part of the directive. For example, Module Plot2D imports only Point2D and PointPolar from the Module Geometry:

```
module Geometry {
    import Algebra;
    export Geo2D, Geo3D;
    language Geo2D {
        syntax Point = '(' Numbers.Number ',' Numbers.Number ')';
        syntax PointPolar = '<' Numbers.Number ',' Numbers.Number '>';
    }
    language Geo3D {
```

```
            syntax Point =
                '(' Numbers.Number ',' Numbers.Number ',' Numbers.Number ')';
        }
    }
    module Plot2D {
        import Geometry {Geo2D};
        language Paths {
            syntax Path = '(' Geo2D.Point* ')';
            syntax PathPolar = '(' Geo2D.PointPolar* ')';
        }
    }
```

An *ImportDirective* that contains an *ImportMember* imports only the named declarations from that module. This means that the following is a compilation error because module `Plot3D` references `Geo3D` which is not imported from module `Geometry`:

```
    module Plot3D {
        import Geometry {Geo2D};
        language Paths {
            syntax Path = '(' Geo3D.Point* ')';
        }
    }
```

An *ImportDirective* that contains an *ImportAlias* on a selected imported member assigns the replacement name to the imported declaration, hiding the original export name.

```
    module Plot3D {
        import Geometry {Geo3D as geo};
        language Paths {
            syntax Path = '(' geo.Point* ')';
        }
    }
```

Aliasing an individual imported member is useful to resolve occasional conflicts between imports. Aliasing an entire imported module is useful to resolve a systemic conflict. For example, when importing two modules, where one is a different version of the other, it is likely to get many conflicts. Aliasing at member level would lead to a correspondingly long list of alias declarations.

CHAPTER 14

ATTRIBUTES

Attributes provide metadata that can be used to interpret the language feature they modify.

AttributeSections:

   AttributeSection

   AttributeSections AttributeSection

AttributeSection:

   @{ *Nodes* }

14.1 Case Sensitive

The `CaseSensitive` attribute controls whether tokens are matched with or without case sensitivity. The default value is `true`. The following language recognizes `"Hello World"`, `"HELLO World"`, and `"hELLO WorLD"`.

```
module HelloWorld {
    @{CaseSensitive[false]}
    language HelloWorld {
        syntax Main
          = Hello World;
        token Hello
          = "Hello";
        token World
          = "World";
        interleave Whitespace
          = " ";
    }
}
```

183

GLOSSARY

abstract   An abstract type describes properties common to many other types but cannot itself be represented.

alias   An alias is a local name for a symbol defined in another module. An alias may be specified on an import.

ambiguity   An ambiguity results when the language processor cannot uniquely determine which of several constructors to run for a given segment of text because the segment is recognized by more than one production. The competing productions do not have to be in the same rule. Ambiguities are resolved by refactoring the grammar and applying precedence directives.

apply   A computed value is applied to its arguments to yield a new value.

arity   Arity is the number of arguments a computed value requires.

ascribe   Ascribing a type to a value requires that the value conform to the type and exposes the behaviors defined on that type.

binding   A pattern may be ascribed with a named variable scoped to the production. When that pattern matches a section of text, that section of text is bound to the variable for use the constructor.

collection   A collection is a container for zero or more values. The values in a collection are called elements. The same value may occur in a collection multiple times but have no order. This is also known as a bag or multiset.

comment   A comment is a sequence of characters in a compilation unit that is excluded from semantic analysis.

compilation unit   A compilation unit is an ordered sequence of Unicode characters that conform to the lexical and grammatical requirements.

concrete   A concrete type can be represented.

conflict	A conflict results whenever the language processor faces a choice in what action to take on a section of text. There are two sorts of conflicts: shift-reduce and reduce-reduce. Not all conflicts result in ambiguities because some conflicts are resolved by applying precedence directives and some conflicts are local. A local conflict means that the language processor faces multiple choices on a section of text, but in a larger context only one collection of choices recognizes the text.
conform	Text conforms to a language if the text matches the Main rule.
constraint	A constraint is a logical test to determine if an element is a member of a collection.
constructor	A constructor defines the output for a production.
context-free	Context-free is a term from computer science to designate a class of languages. All languages in this class can be written with a single non-terminal on the left-hand side of the rule and can be recognized with a push-down automaton.
declaration	A declaration binds a symbol to a type or computed value.
default	A default is a value to be used unless no other is specified.
derived	A derived type is constraint over some other type.
dynamic	A dynamic quality is any quality that is not static.
element	An element is a value in a collection.
entity	An entity is a set of labeled values.
export	An export makes a symbol visible outside the module in which it was declared. It is not visible within another module unless it is imported.
expression	An expression is a sequence of Unicode characters that conforms to the Expression production in the grammar. In general it consists of an operator and one or more operands. Applying the operator to the operand yields a new value.
extent	An extent is a location that holds a value at the module scope.
field	A field is a location that holds a value at the entity scope.
grammar	A grammar is a set of rules that determine if a sequence of characters conform to a language. As used in the specification, these rules are context-free.

identifier   An identifier is a symbolic name for use in a program. Type names, formal parameters, module names, and names of computed values are all examples of identifiers.

identity   Identity is a value that implies equality between entities. The identity value can be used as a surrogate for the entity itself as in a reference.

import   An import makes a symbol visible outside the module in which it was declared visible within the module containing the import.

initializer   An initializer in an expression that returns a collection or entity value.

instance   An instance is a value that conforms to an entity type.

interleave   Designating a rule interleave separates the sections of text recognized by the rule from normal language processing. These are used to define insignificant whitespace and comment rules.

intrinsic   Intrinsic definitions are part of the language and cannot be added to or extended by a library.

language   A language is a collection of rules potentially with a designated Main rule. If the language has a Main rule, and a text value matches that rule, then the text value conforms to the language or is recognized by the language. In this case, the output of the rule is the output of the language.

lexical   A lexical rule determines if a sequence of characters conform to a language. As used in this specification, lexical rules are regular expressions, and ambiguity is resolved by taking the longest match.

library   A library is an informal name for a commonly used collection of declarations.

literal   A literal is a sequence of characters that represent a simple value.

member   A member is a field or computed value within an entity scope.

module   A module is a unit of encapsulation.

nominal type   Values in a nominal type system names the types they are members of. Also, subtypes name their supertypes.

null   The value null is a distinct value that is used as a placeholder.

operand	An operand is an expression used as an argument to an operator.
operator	An operator is a character or sequence of characters that is used in an expression to denote a computed value.
overloading	Overloading is giving the same symbol multiple interpretations within the same scope. The only form of overloading in M is on the number of arguments to a computed value.
parser	A parser is a language processor.
pattern	A pattern occurs on the left side of a production and recognizes text and potentially binds the text to a variable.
precedence	Precedence is a statement of preference between two choices available to the language processor.
prefix	A prefix is a section of a text value from the beginning of the value to an arbitrary point. Both the empty value and the whole text value are prefixes of a text value.
pre-processing	Pre-processing includes or excludes portions of a compilation unit as determined by pre-processing directives.
production	A production consists of a pattern and an optional constructor.
program	A program is a collection of compilation units that conform to the lexical, grammatical, and semantic rules of the language.
projector	A projector yields a new collection with one member from all the elements in a source collection.
query	A query is an expression that yields a new collection from one or more input collections.
recognize	A language recognizes a text value if it matches the Main rule.
reduce-reduce	A reduce-reduce conflict occurs if two rules match the same section of text. It may be resolved using precedence.
reference	A reference holds the identity value of another entity.
regular	Regular is a term from computer science for a class of languages. It is a subclass of the context-free languages in which the rules are tail recursive and can be recognized by a finite-state automation.
representation	A representation is a storage format for a value. Typically a representation will restrict precision or stipulate an encoding.

rule	A rule is a collection of productions with an optional name. There are three forms of rules: syntax, token, and interleave.
scope	Scope is the range in which a symbol is defined within the source text. A scope is a container for symbol declarations. In M scopes are lexical, which means they can be determined from the block structure of the language (unless otherwise specified).
selector	A selector yields a new collection containing all the elements of a source collection with a member equal to a value given as an argument.
set	A collection of distinct elements.
shift-reduce	A shift-reduce conflict occurs when the language processor can take different actions on two productions or within a single production. It may be resolved using precedence.
start rule	The start rule is the first rule a language processor attempts to match when recognizing a text value. The start rule for Mg is named Main.
static	A static quality is any quality that can be determined by reviewing the source text alone.
storage	A location that holds a value (see field and extent).
structural type	A type whose membership is determined by satisfying a structural pattern and possibly other constraints.
subtype	A subtype, S, is a type that permits only values of some other type, T.
supertype	A supertype, T, is a type that permits all of the values of some other type, S.
symbol	A symbol is an identifier in the source text. Symbols are defined within scopes. Modules control the visibility of symbols.
syntax	Syntax is used in two ways. In the general sense, syntax is the rules that define a language. In Mg, syntax is used to designate a rule that defines a context-free language.
token	Token is used to designate a rule that defines a regular language. It is also used to name the sections of a text value recognized by such a rule.
type	A type is a predicate over values that yields a collection.

unique

An element is unique within a collection if no other element is equal to it.

value

Syntactically, a value is and expression constructed solely from literals and initializers. It contains no variable reverences, computed values, or operators. Conceptually a value is any abstract notion that can be represented in this way.

variable

A variable is a symbolic name for value.

Microsoft .NET Development Series

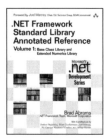

.NET Framework Standard Library Annotated Reference
Volume 1: Base Class Library and Extended Numerics Library

Brad Abrams

978-0-321-15489-7

.NET Framework Standard Library Annotated Reference
Volume 2: Networking Library, Reflection Library and XML Library

Brad Abrams
Tamara Abrams

978-0-321-19445-9

Essential Windows Presentation Foundation

Chris Anderson

978-0-321-37447-9

A Developer's Guide to SQL Server 2005

Bob Beauchemin
Dan Sullivan

978-0-321-38218-4

Advanced ASP.NET AJAX Server Controls
For .NET Framework 3.5

Adam Calderon
Joel Rumerman

978-0-321-51444-8

Visual Studio Tools for Office
Using C# with Excel, Word, Outlook, and InfoPath

Eric Carter
Eric Lippert

978-0-321-33488-6

Visual Studio Tools for Office
Using Visual Basic 2005 with Excel, Word, Outlook, and InfoPath

Eric Carter
Eric Lippert

978-0-321-41175-4

Domain-Specific Development
with Visual Studio DSL Tools

Steve Cook
Gareth Jones
Stuart Kent
Alan Cameron Wills

978-0-321-39820-8

Software Engineering with Microsoft Visual Studio Team System

Sam Guckenheimer
with Juan J. Perez

978-0-321-27872-2

The C# Programming Language
Third Edition

Anders Hejlsberg
Mads Torgersen
Scott Wiltamuth
Peter Golde

978-0-321-56299-9

ASP.NET 2.0 Illustrated

Alex Homer
Dave Sussman

978-0-321-41834-0

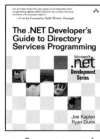

The .NET Developer's Guide to Directory Services Programming

Joe Kaplan
Ryan Dunn

978-0-321-35017-6

Smart Client Deployment with ClickOnce
Deploying Windows Forms Applications with ClickOnce

Brian Noyes

978-0-321-19769-6

Essential ASP.NET 2.0

Fritz Onion
with Keith Brown

978-0-321-23770-5

Essential Windows Communication Foundation
For .NET Framework 3.5

Steve Resnick
Richard Crane
Chris Bowen

978-0-321-44006-8

.NET Internationalization
The Developer's Guide to Building Global Windows and Web Applications

Guy Smith-Ferrier

978-0-321-34138-9

Visual Studio Team System
Better Software Development for Agile Teams

Will Stott
James Newkirk

978-0-321-41850-0

Essential .NET
Volume 1
The Common Language Runtime

Don Box
with Chris Sells

978-0-201-73411-9

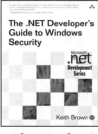

The .NET Developer's
Guide to Windows
Security

Keith Brown

978-0-321-22835-2

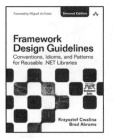

Framework
Design Guidelines
Conventions, Idioms, and Patterns
for Reusable .NET Libraries

Krzysztof Cwalina
Brad Abrams

978-0-321-54561-9

Concurrent
Programming
on Windows

Joe Duffy

978-0-321-43482-1

Effective Use of Microsoft
Enterprise Library
Building Blocks for Creating
Enterprise Applications and Services

Len Fenster

978-0-321-33421-3

Essential C# 3.0
For .NET Framework 3.5

Mark Michaelis

978-0-321-53392-0

The
Common Language
Infrastructure
Annotated Standard

James S. Miller
Susann Ragsdale

978-0-321-15493-4

Enterprise Services
with the .NET
Framework
Developing Distributed Business
Solutions with .NET Enterprise Services

Christian Nagel

978-0-321-24673-8

Data Binding with
Windows Forms 2.0
Programming Smart Client
Data Applications with .NET

Brian Noyes

978-0-321-26892-1

Designing Forms for
Microsoft Office InfoPath
and Forms Services 2007

Scott Roberts
Hagen Green

978-0-321-41059-7

eXtreme .NET
Introducing eXtreme Programming
Techniques to .NET Developers

Dr. Neil Roodyn

978-0-321-30363-9

Windows Forms 2.0
Programming

Chris Sells
Michael Weinhardt

978-0-321-26796-2

Essential Windows
Workflow Foundation

Dharma Shukla
Bob Schmidt

978-0-321-39983-0

The Visual Basic
.NET Programming
Language

Paul Vick

978-0-321-16951-8

.NET Compact
Framework Programming
with C#

Paul Yao
David Durant

978-0-321-17403-1

.NET Compact
Framework Programming
with Visual Basic .NET

Paul Yao
David Durant

978-0-321-17404-8

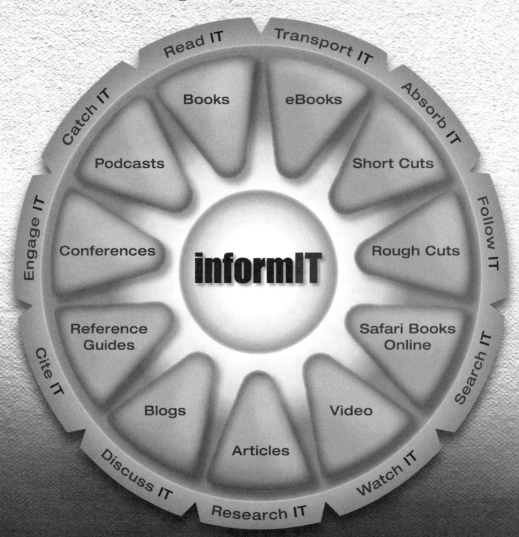

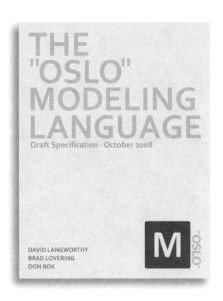

FREE Online Edition

Your purchase of **The "Oslo" Modeling Language Draft Specification - October 2008** includes access to a free online edition for 45 days through the Safari Books Online subscription service. Nearly every Sams book is available online through Safari Books Online, along with over 5,000 other technical books and videos from publishers such as Cisco Press, Exam Cram, IBM Press, O'Reilly, Prentice Hall, Que, and Sams.

SAFARI BOOKS ONLINE allows you to search for a specific answer, cut and paste code, download chapters, and stay current with emerging technologies.

Activate your FREE Online Edition at
www.informit.com/safarifree

> **STEP 1:** Enter the coupon code: ULTJSAA.

> **STEP 2:** New Safari users, complete the brief registration form.
> Safari subscribers, just login.

If you have difficulty registering on Safari or accessing the online edition, please e-mail customer-service@safaribooksonline.com